Greater Works

And How to perform Miracles

By Jeff Lowe

www.xulonpress.com

Dedications:

This book is dedicated to all the believers who have been faithful doing the works of Jesus throughout the years. It is also dedicated to God's miracle army of Prophets, Apostles and the believers who will catch the vision and run with it.

Acknowledgements:

For all the inspiration and encouragement: Pastors Bayless and Janet Conley, Pastor Kenneth Mulkey, Dr. Chris and Robin Harfouce, Tree of Life Ministry Partners all over the world, my ever interceding parents; Herman and Karen Lowe and my beautiful wife Shen'na.

Table of Contents

INTRODUCTION

S alvation was not meant to be a final destination, but a beginning. The greatest miracle that God can do is to change you. He wants to inspire your mind and draw you into the intimacy of a relationship with His loving Spirit. Many people witnessed and received miracles of Jesus and the apostles, but went away empty in their souls. You may have gone to a church many times and have come away empty handed. You may have been preached religion instead of the Kingdom of God. It is because you are so valuable to God that He wants to shape your mind into His. This book carries the Presence of God to impart your destiny for you to think like God. It is not a *'cookie-cutter'* formula, but a commissioning insight to combine with your individual God given talents. It will give you the faith to awaken who you really are. You are called to heal the multitudes like Jesus and glorify His Kingdom, but first you need the how to.

"For whom he did foreknow, he also did predestinate to be conformed to the image of his Son..." Romans 8:29

"But we all, with open face beholding as in a glass the glory of the Lord, are changed into the same image from glory to glory, even as by the Spirit of the LORD." 2 Corinthians 3:18

"Because of this, we also, from the day we heard, do not cease on behalf for you offering our petitions and presenting our definite requests, that you might be filled with the advanced and perfect experiential knowledge of his will in the sphere of every kind of wisdom and intelligence which is spiritual" Colossians 1:9 KW

This book will direct you to scripture and help you exercise the ability, authority, power and dominion that God has given you. There will be a few things that you may be well versed in, but I am led to go over a few basics as I have found many people who read my books around the world have not been fully taught the character and gospel of the Kingdom. I also use a lot of scripture so readers and hearers don't have to use or give too much value to opinions. Some scriptures that are repeated have amplified or expanded translations for further insight. The bible is like a mirror to see your-self endowed with His promise of abundant life. We have learned what not to do with life, including the promptings of our own conscious, but we need to reach out to God and open up our minds to work in its full capacity. We all need to have our minds to be fertile ground for the deposit of His seed. We can see that religion (*man's way to God*) is a substitute for the relationship (*God's way to man*) of the Kingdom of God.

This book is not about '*church*' business but kingdom business. I don't teach in a pastoral function to take care of the sheep or baby them, but as an apostle to train soldiers and warriors. Although many who are there to please people or gain members for their own desires or gain are cut off like Saul, God is raising up many pastors to include prophetic and apostolic functions to build His kingdom. You can choose to follow the crowds, organizations, mediocre or popular teaching like the rebellious children of Israel with Korah (Numbers 16) or be a pioneer and enter into the land of promises like Caleb and Joshua. We may have started in the dry places but the Kingdom life is our destiny.

When you see God in the vision of this book, you will value it to change your life and others around you. You don't need to be infallible, but know that the infallible one lives in you. You will get the information for meditation unto illumination to activation and manifestation. God is more real than this book in your hands and is personably able to confirm the truths in this book.

"For this is good and acceptable in the sight of God our Saviour; Who will have all men to be saved, and to come unto the knowledge of the truth." 1 Timothy 2:3, 4

"All scripture is given by inspiration of God, and is profitable for doctrine, for reproof, for correction, for instruction in righteousness. That the man of God may be perfect, throughly furnished unto all good works." 2 Timothy 3:16, 17

"Search the scriptures; for in them ye think ye have eternal life: and they are they which testify of me." John 5:39

Chapter 1

A Greater Power

Your calling is to prepare how to live with God and His people for an eternity. By using the Word to restore, rescue and reconcile, you will do greater works for the kingdom. God is activating you to be a champion on behalf of His kingdom. Even the seeds you are reading right now are seeds planted by God for direct deposit into your spirit. You are being supernaturally charged with heavenly instructions for an earthly battle of faith in a 'fixed' fight. You have answered the call of God. You have chosen to be chosen. You will ignore the devil, circumstances and self-led people, for continuous, guaranteed victory. You will go from thinking about having a visitation, to knowing you are a habitation. Your acceleration of revelation will lead to manifestation, and a revival that the world has never seen before.

"This mystery has been kept in the dark for a long time, but now it's out in the open. God wanted everyone, not just Jews, to know this rich and glorious secret inside and out, regardless of their background, regardless of their religious standing. The mystery in a nutshell is just this: Christ is in you, so therefore you can look forward

to sharing in God's glory. It's that simple. That is the substance of our Message." Colossians 1:26, 27 MB

God is giving you His faith. There are times when a greater power than yourself will come upon you. He wants us all to plug into this power He gave us to do greater things. If you don't believe in His available goals, you will not be conformed to the image and do what He does. You will fall short of His glory and fall into the rituals of religion instead of relationship. If you've 'tried' praying and were not absolute about the outcome or wavered and did not hold onto the truth of the Word because of impatience, you can continue to read and get ready to increase your faith from ordinary observation and earthly expectation to the confidence in His continuous confirmation for you.

"Jesus said to him, "If you can believe, all things *are* possible to him who believes. Immediately the father of the child cried out and said with tears, "Lord, I believe; help my unbelief!" Mark 9:23, 24 NKJ

"But let patience have *its* perfect work, that you may be perfect and complete, lacking nothing. If any of you lacks wisdom, let him ask of God, who gives to all liberally and without reproach, and it will be given to him. But let him ask in faith, with no doubting, for he who doubts is like a wave of the sea driven and tossed by the wind. For let not that man suppose that he will receive anything from the Lord; *he is* a double-minded man, unstable in all his ways." James 1:4-8 NKJ

Perhaps a wavering minister or relative imparted a God who '*used-to-do-it*' spirit or '*not-for-you*' spirit in your life. You are ready to let go of the yesterday's that have lied to you, the mediocrity of spiritual '*good-enough-to-get-by*' snacks, or yesterday's '*stale bread*' into the inheritance of a blood bought living pathway of daily 'full course meals' for the provision to feed multitudes. Although we may be infallible creatures, the un-infallible one lives in us to give us this high calling and guides us if we miss the mark;

"Not as though I had already attained, either were already perfect: but I follow after, if that I may apprehend that for which also I am apprehended of Christ Jesus. Brethren, I count not myself to have apprehended: but this one thing I do, forgetting those things which are behind, and reaching forth unto those things which are before, I press toward the mark for the prize of the high calling of God in Christ Jesus. Let us therefore, as many as be perfect, be thus minded: and if in any thing ye be otherwise minded, God shall reveal even this unto you."
Philippians 3:12-15

Sometimes in life, people are so caught up in fantasy, that the Truth becomes fantasy to them. We've all read about the power we can have and yet, our minds have settled for the temporal fantasies of the world, or looked at the mediocrity others have accepted and set that bar as a standard. These are temporary expressions of the *world system* that are designed to make you fail. They are doctrines of demons that have been preached through men for thousands of years. It takes time to demolish what the *world system* has set up. Many nations have been in poverty for hundreds of years, but it takes understanding, belief and speaking a Word to defy years of poverty. Many nations have suffered from diseases, but God's unchanging Truth and desire are still the same.

Now that our hearts are conforming to the mind of Jesus, we are letting go of powerless attitudes, fantasies of selfish superstardom, covetous thinking, and unhealthy daydreams of the opposite sex and cutting off fellowship with life draining unbelievers. We seek and find mentors and people who actually let the unwavering mind of Christ stay in them.

"And there was a great famine in Samaria: and, behold, they besieged it, until an ass's head was sold for fourscore pieces of silver, and the fourth part of a cab of dove's dung for five pieces of silver. Then Elisha said, Hear ye the word of the LORD; Thus saith the LORD, To morrow about this time shall a measure of fine flour be sold for a shekel, and two measures of barley for a shekel, in the gate of Samaria." 2 Kings 6:25, 7:1

We will live and give off the Truth we receive. Our flow of music, literature and inspired speaking helps keep us attached to the constant flow of the Spirit. Only a relationship with God will develop the anointing. The signs will only follow them that believe. We renew ourselves with the habitual meditation of who we are in God, our heavenly identity and authority to be a benefit to others. We are here to be proof providers of a resurrected Savior and to uncover the unlimited power that has sat dormant within us. We shouldn't be full of God and keep it to ourselves.

"Then another came, saying, 'Master, here is your mina, which I have kept put away in a handkerchief. For I feared you, because you are an austere man. You collect what you did not deposit, and reap what you did not sow.' And he said to him, 'Out of your own mouth I will judge you, *you* wicked servant. You knew that I was an austere man, collecting what I did not deposit and reaping what I did not sow." Luke 19:20-22 NKJ

"Do not be unequally yoked together with unbelievers. For what fellowship has righteousness with lawless-

ness? And what communion has light with darkness?"
2 Corinthians 6:14 NKJ

"Mark the perfect man, and behold the upright: for the
end of that man is peace." Psalm 37:37

"Let your gentleness be known unto all men. The Lord is
at hand." Philippians 4:5 NKJ

To have this intimacy, you must be a 'God hunter'. We
have started with a faith in someone who we have never seen
before. Faith grows when we find out about His nature of
love, compassion and willingness to improve our lives in
this world and in this time. We get used to that ever present
'still small voice'. It is that peaceful impression that connects
you with blessings or divine appointments. Sometimes the
voice gets a little louder to keep us from danger, like a father
protecting his children. It will always be backed up by his
written word and give us intimate confidence for the prosperity He has for us.

"But without faith it is impossible to please him: for he
that cometh to God must believe that he is, and that he is a
rewarder of them that diligently seek him." Hebrews 11:6

"My sheep hear my voice, and I know them, and they
follow me" John 10:27

"Beloved, I pray that you may prosper in all things and be
in health, just as your soul prospers." 3 John 1:2 NKJ

Get ready to take all the limits off of your life. There are
more reports of healing, miracles and creative miracles these
days, than we've ever seen on the planet. With the power
of God, people have recently grown legs, eyeballs, heart

valves, have been raised from the dead and so much more. It is the will of the Father for us to be immediately healed. You want it now, He wanted it yesterday. We are catching up to his timeless desire of promises. We are realizing He wants to openly display His mercy in this life instead of judgment. When your spiritual intimacy with God increases to the revelation of His preferred timing, your speed will be according to the 'right now' faith. As with any relationship, our availability, or favorable awareness of His presence will increase with time. He will reveal Himself to us;

"Therefore submit to God. Resist the devil and he will flee from you. Draw near to God and He will draw near to you. Cleanse *your* hands, *you* sinners; and purify *your* hearts, *you* double-minded." James 4:7, 8

As you climb this ladder of faith of believing and expectancy, you will not only realize that this same power will become evident in you, but you will also be a pioneering example to teach others to come off the bench of idleness. Jesus did not only come here to give us a ticket to everlasting life, but to let his powerful will be done on earth, as it is in heaven through you. Virtually everything that Jesus did can operate in you. We are here to pick up the spoils the enemy has forfeited.

"...Thy will be done in earth, as it is in heaven." Matthew 6:10

"When a strong man, fully armed, guards his own palace, his goods are in peace. But when a stronger than he comes upon him and overcomes him, he takes from him all his armor in which he trusted, and divides his spoils. He who is not with Me is against Me, and he who does not gather with Me scatters." Luke 11:21-23 NKJ

Every enemy, every spirit of infirmity knows we have authority over them. The problem in the past is that we didn't know better. In former times we may have blamed God for being an accessory to things gone wrong in our lives to teach us a lesson, as if the Spirit would not teach us all things. We are learning that disease has no purpose or authority to exist in our lives. We may have had more faith in our observances, emotions or impatience, thinking God works in *'mysterious ways'* or the *'let us have it how we want it and when we want it'* attitude, but the Word of God is more powerful than what we think. It took a spiritually mature person to move us out of the *'baby stroller'* of *'give me what I demand'* to driving the vehicle of faith to give our circle of influence a ride to freedom. For us creatures who are born walking by sight and not by faith, it took God to move in on us and a minister to speak *His name* and impart *His nature* in us into an authoritative expectancy of who we are, what we are called to do and what our enemy is up to;

**"And His disciples asked Him, saying, "Rabbi, who sinned, this man or his parents, that he was born blind? Jesus answered, Neither this man nor his parents sinned, but that the works of God should be revealed in him."
John 9:2, 3**

"But go and learn what *this* means: *'I desire mercy and not sacrifice ...'"* Matthew 9:13

"But the mercy of the LORD is from everlasting to everlasting upon them that fear him, and his righteousness unto children's children" Psalm 103:17

"Behold, I give unto you power to tread on serpents and scorpions, and over all the power of the enemy: and nothing shall by any means hurt you." Luke 10:19

"Lest Satan should get an advantage of us: for we are not ignorant of his devices." 2 Corinthians 2:11

We are here to pick up the spoils that the enemy has left behind. Gathering the spoils is the ability to take control of any situation in regards to your thought life for God given spiritual empowerment. The devil is well aware of this and knows you have authority over him. He recognizes the voice of God in you and knows his dominion is over. Stronger demons may do a spiritual background check, but your consistent submission to God and resilience in the anointing will see them flee.

God is now placing a demand on the anointing within the Seed that He has placed within you. He has a mighty army of angels to back up His Word with presence and performance. Become God conscious instead of sin conscious. You will experience what you believe. The greater power invested in you will reap great rewards.

"Awake to righteousness, and sin not; for some have not the knowledge of God: I speak this to your shame." 1 Corinthians 15:34

"You prepare a table before me in the presence of my enemies. You anoint my head with oil; my [brimming] cup runs over. Surely or only goodness, mercy, and unfailing love shall follow me all the days of my life, and through the length of my days the house of the Lord [and His presence] shall be my dwelling place." Psalm 23:5, 6 AMP

CHAPTER 2

Prayer

There are many books on prayer, but I want to share some things in this chapter that I don't find mentioned in them. Simply put, prayer is communication or the exchange of ideas and information with the Spirit of God. We should constantly be in prayer even if it is in the conversation of another believer or potential believer. We may easily speak thousands of words on a daily basis, but God's *direction* is ever present when we are still and ready to receive. Your faith will allow God to talk to you. He speaks many impressions expressed with His gentle Spirit and will preach to you if you can be patient to receive it. He will direct you to your own miracle.

"Pray without ceasing." 1 Thessalonians 5:17

"Do not rash with your mouth, and let not your heart utter anything hastily before God. For God is in heaven, and you on earth; Therefore let your words be few. For a dream comes through much activity, and a fool's voice *is known* by *his* many words." Ecclesiastes 5:2, 3 NKJ

"I will instruct you and teach you in the way you should go; I will guide you with My eye." Psalm 32:8

"In all your ways acknowledge Him, and He shall direct your paths." Proverbs 3:6 NKJ

The source of the unwavering prayer of faith comes from God. Our confidence is built when we hear and read more Word. This results in our identity of the power resident within us. He gives us an impression of what to ask for, or someone asks us to intercede about something we are sure that lines up with His will. We can repeat His words back to Him in agreement of the Word that our minds have listened to. You may have to fast or consecrate (*stay away from worldly things so that you can be in touch with the abundance of revelation God has for you*) to focus and fine tune your prayer life. When you learn God knows your intentions, there is realization that the Spirit will intercede for your mistakes. Your words will carry the presence of God. He will answer your prayer better than you can ask it.

"And Jesus answering saith unto them, Have faith in God." Mark 11:22

"But let him ask in faith, with no doubting, for he who doubts is like a wave of the sea driven and tossed by the wind. For let not that man suppose that he will receive anything from the Lord." James 1:6, 7 NKJ

"And when he was come into the house, his disciples asked him privately, Why could not we cast him out? And he said unto them, This kind can come forth by nothing, but by prayer and fasting." Mark 9:28, 29

"Likewise the Spirit also helps in our weaknesses. For we do not know what we should pray for as we ought, but the Spirit Himself makes intercession for us with groanings which cannot be uttered. Now He who searches the hearts knows what the mind of the Spirit *is,* because He makes intercession for the saints according to *the will of God.*" Romans 8:26, 27 NKJ

"God can do anything, you know far more than you could ever imagine or guess or request in your wildest dreams! He does it not by pushing us around but by working within us, his Spirit deeply and gently within us." Ephesians 3:20, 21 MB

When you receive the revelation of who you are in God and how precious and valuable you are to Him, you become more confident in prayer. When Jesus took His own blood as a sacrifice to a heaven that was stained with the sin of the former angel Lucifer, it gave us direct access to God. There is no more '*work*' we need to do to get prayer answered. When Jesus said it is finished, it *was* finished. Our communion lost by the fall of Adam was restored. He gave His life to send his comforting Spirit of fellowship. We are made righteous by the blood of Jesus and justified, just as if we've never sinned. He never has to pay that price again. He cherishes you and directs you in prayer.

"Let us therefore come boldly unto the throne of grace, that we may obtain mercy, and find grace to help in time of need." Hebrews 4:16

"Nevertheless I tell you the truth. It is to your advantage that I go away; for if I do not go away, the Helper will not come to you; but if I depart, I will send Him to you." John 16:7 NKJ

"...and whom he called, them he also justified: and whom he justified, them he also glorified...He that spared not his own Son, but delivered him up for us all, how shall he not with him also freely give us all things?" Romans 8:30, 32

Our confidence grows when we know His will and promises. Even if the enemy is not accusing us, sometimes our heart will attempt to condemn us because of generations of accusational teachings installed in us instead of God's teaching of freedom. When we pray we don't acknowledge any sinful past, even if it was a few minutes ago. God's word and blood separates them. He is not out to punish us, but loves us enough to separate us from extreme evil as He did with Noah and Lot, and what He will do in a future rapture and eternity. Our previous choices may have missed the mark, and may have resulted in unfavorable consequences, but we should not punish ourselves by thinking that we cannot come to our Father at anytime. We are not to be self-righteous because pride will not accept what it doesn't earn. Works has never been the way to God unless it's the works of believing Him. His sacrifice; your benefit. His pain; your gain.

In His sight He allowed us to be perfect, pure, and holy, to love ourselves and others. He knows we can. He gives us power to renew our minds and learn how to do so.

"For all the promises of God in him are yea, and in him Amen, unto the glory of God by us." 2 Corinthians 1:20

"For I am persuaded, that neither death, nor life, nor angels, nor principalities, nor powers, nor things present, nor things to come, Nor height, nor depth, nor any other creature, shall be able to separate us from the love of God, which is in Christ Jesus our Lord." Romans 8:38, 39

"Be ye therefore perfect, even as your Father which is in heaven is perfect." Matthew 5:48

"Unto the pure all things are pure: but unto them that are defiled and unbelieving is nothing pure..." Titus 1:15

"but as He who called you *is* holy, you also be holy in all *your* conduct, because it is written, *"Be holy, for I am holy."* 1 Peter 1:15, 16 NKJ

"And by this we know that we are of the truth, and shall assure our hearts before Him. For if our heart condemns us, God is greater than our heart, and knows all things. Beloved, if our heart does not condemn us, we have confidence toward God. And whatever we ask we receive from Him, because we keep His commandments and do those things that are pleasing in His sight. And this is His commandment: that we should believe on the name of His Son Jesus Christ and love one another, as He gave us commandment." 1 John 3:19-23 NKJ

"And be not conformed to this world: but be ye transformed by the renewing of your mind, that ye may prove what is that good, and acceptable, and perfect, will of God." Romans 12:2

You will experience your life according to your perception of God. There must be a death to the old way of thinking (*with our flesh, or carnal mind*). He is love and only can love. In His consistency we are completely eternally blameless to Him. His beauty has made you beautiful. You are as blameless to Him as a little baby is to us. How you think He sees you will let you remain confident in your innocence given by grace. The revelation of innocence comes by acknowledging there isn't the slightest contamination of a sense of

27

separation from the total acceptance of God. He acknowl-edges your born again spirit as your only true identity. This makes you have confidence in prayer. This takes you from '*I think I am*' to 'I know I am' We go from *sin-conscious-ness* to God-consciousness that is clear and free from guilt. You start to think like God and not like man.

"Everyone who confesses that Jesus is God's Son partici-pates continuously in an intimate relationship with God. We know it so well, we've embraced it heart and soul, this love that comes from God." 1 John 4:15, 16 MB

"Even when we were dead in trespasses, made us alive together with Christ (by grace you have been saved), and raised *us* up together, and made *us* sit together in the heavenly *places* in Christ Jesus" Ephesians 2:5, 6 NKJ

"The Spirit of the Lord GOD is upon me...to proclaim liberty to the captives, and the opening of the prison to them that are bound. To appoint unto them that mourn in Zion, to give unto them beauty for ashes...that they might be called trees of righteousness, the planting of the LORD, that he might be glorified." Isaiah 61:1, 3

"When I was a child, I spake as a child, I understood as a child, I thought as a child: but when I became a man, I put away childish things." 1 Corinthians 13:11

"For ye are dead, and your life is hid with Christ in God." Colossians 3:3

We mature beyond praying for ourselves and success-fully intercede when see other Christians as innocent as God does. We want to encourage others that pray with us of their right-standing with God. We don't want to encourage the self-destruction of others by agreeing that they are weak, sick, poor or lost and can't do anything about it. We want all of our prayers to be a benefit to the body of Christ.

"...let the weak say, I am strong." Joel 3:10

"...but God's Word isn't in jail!" 2 Timothy 2:9 MB

"Be prepared. You're up against far more than you can handle on your own. Take all the help you can get, every weapon God has issued, so that when it's all over but the shouting you'll still be on your feet. Truth, righteousness, peace, faith, and salvation are more than words. Learn how to apply them. You'll need them throughout your life. God's Word is an indispensable weapon. In the same way, prayer is essential in this ongoing warfare. Pray hard and long. Pray for your brothers and sisters. Keep your eyes open." Ephesians 6:17, 18 MB

Prayer works. When you want to change your atmosphere; pray for divine appointments and opportunities. Get together in agreement with others. Avoid skeptics and opposing people, whether leaders or laymen. Ask that God teaches you how to flow in His gift of life that He gave you. Pray for areas of things that are not in agreement with what the Word says you should have. Move the things you see in life beyond sight into the invisible and unchangeable. Prayer changes things. If you don't like it, you can change it. Every born again voice is important. Pray with the authority, power that God invested in you. Believe in mighty things. God can protect individuals and families like He protected the children of Israel. Press into the yes and Amen of God. The body of Christ will have a cooperate experience like Israel and see the promised land (*still fighting, but winning*).

The move of God happens with us. Prayer is the key that unlocks the door for God to intervene. Let your ability to speak become wings and break the chains off the body of Christ. Let your reputation become that which others can call on you for.

"....traitors, headstrong, haughty, lovers of pleasure rather than lovers of God, [5] having a form of godliness but denying its power. And from such people turn away!" 2 Timothy 3:4, 5 NKJ

"So I say to you, ask, and it will be given to you; seek, and you will find; knock, and it will be opened to you." Luke 11:9 NKJ

"There are, it may be, so many kinds of voices in the world, and none of them is without signification." 1 Corinthians 14:10

"Samuel grew up. God was with him, and Samuel's prophetic record was flawless. Everyone in Israel, from Dan in the north to Beersheba in the south, recognized that Samuel was the real thing; a true prophet of God." 1 Samuel 3:19, 20

CHAPTER 3

Our Calling

God has called all of His creation to be saved from darkness. He wants us to spend time with Him and learn His strategy of bringing men to this same truth. He wants us to teach the Kingdom of God to free His people from every yoke of bondage. The knowledge of our heavenly identity and authority that He has given us will cause us to do greater works in Christ.

God has validated you. It has been said; 'God doesn't call the qualified, He qualifies the called'. You are selected to have the faith that enforces the power of God. You will take the steps of edification, revelation, elevation, impartation and activation to be a witness for God. Your perception of your spiritual conception will give you reception to be an exception to current Holy Spirit rejection. You are called to heal multitudes and have been granted the power to do so. When you learn how to harness the power, or flow with God given direction by making the Word alive with the Spirit, you will make great use of your spiritual inheritance. You are God's beneficiary to receive and deliver what has been available since time began. You have the spiritual power of attorney over sickness and diseases.

"And Jesus answering saith unto them, Have faith in God." Mark 11:22

"But ye shall receive power, after that the Holy Ghost is come upon you: and ye shall be witnesses unto me..." Acts 1:

If the only vision you have is the past, you will deteriorate in life and be static at best. Your insight has to be bigger than the things you see and hear about from the world's events around you. The vision refreshes us into contagious hope. If Jude said we must contend for faith in his time, we must do even more above our fellows who are surrounded by churches without power. We must do more than planting powerless churches and doing missionary work and leaving people un-discipled. We must teach them the Kingdom of God. The work of an Evangelist is just the beginning. We don't want to just have a new 'Baby Christian' abandoned at the doorsteps, but continue to disciple them with love *and* power. Many countries in Africa and the Caribbean have too many Indians and not enough Chiefs that teach and demonstrate the power of God. We must teach the complete vision that God has given us.

"Where there is no vision, the people perish..."Proverbs 29:18

"Where there is no vision, the people cast off restraint..." Proverbs 29:18 ASV

"Without prophecy, the people become demoralized..." Proverbs 29:18 NAB

"My people are destroyed for lack of knowledge..." Hosea 4:6

"Dear friends, I've dropped everything to write you about this life of salvation that we have in common. I have to write insisting and begging! that you fight with everything you have in you for this faith entrusted to us as a gift to guard and cherish." Jude 1:3 MB

"Go out and train everyone you meet, far and near, in this way of life, marking them by baptism in the three-fold name: Father, Son, and Holy Spirit. Then instruct them in the practice of all I have commanded you." Matthew 28:18, 19 MB

Follow God. Ask Him for the wisdom you need to fulfill your calling. One of the greatest things that God can deliver you from is your own agenda. The freedom from your self will open a transparent pathway for others to receive from God. You won't have to try so hard to be right, but accept His righteousness and follow His ever present lead. You will win the battleground in your mind that may be doing a commentary on whether or not God's word is true. You can see yourself as a champion in the Word and be the person it says you are *and* do what it says you can do.

"Trust in the LORD with all your heart, And lean not on your own understanding; In all your ways acknowledge Him, And He shall direct your paths." Proverbs 3:5, 6 NKJ

"Examine yourselves *as to* whether you are in the faith. Test yourselves. Do you not know yourselves, that Jesus Christ is in you?—unless indeed you are disqualified" 2 Corinthians 13:5 NKJ

Prepare yourself for an intimate relationship with our Lord. If Jesus physically showed up in the life of the majority of people, they would be in fear. Many religious people do not want that close fellowship with God, whether it was the Israelites telling Moses to represent for them or the chief priests who would rather hold on to their own lifestyle instead of listening to the testimony of the resurrection of Jesus from secular Roman soldiers. When some people see miracles beyond their capacity to receive it, they fear what they don't understand.

"Now all the people witnessed the thunderings, the lightning flashes, the sound of the trumpet, and the mountain smoking; and when the people saw *it,* they trembled and stood afar off. Then they said to Moses, "You speak with us, and we will hear; but let not God speak with us, lest we die." Exodus 20:18, 19 NKJ

"...the angel of the Lord descended from heaven, and came and rolled back the stone from the door, and sat upon it....And for fear of him the keepers did shake, and became as dead men... Now when they were going, behold, some of the watch came into the city, and shewed unto the chief priests all the things that were done. And when they were assembled with the elders, and had taken counsel, they gave large money unto the soldiers..." Matthew 28:2, 4, 11, 12

You may have read many verses in the bible that seemed impossible, or did not appear to apply to you. This is a normal human reaction to the Word as a person or in a book. Many were initially afraid of the unknown like Peter after seeing a miracle, but eventually embraced God's available power and freedom from lifetimes of bondage and condemnation.

"When Simon Peter saw it, he fell down at Jesus' knees, saying, Depart from me; for I am a sinful man, O Lord.

For he was astonished, and all that were with him, at the draught of the fishes which they had taken" Luke 5:8, 9

"And when the disciples saw him walking on the sea, they were troubled, saying, It is a spirit; and they cried out for fear." Matthew 14:26

"And they come to Jesus, and see him that was possessed with the devil, and had the legion, sitting, and clothed, and in his right mind: and they were afraid. And they began to pray him to depart out of their coasts." Mark 5:15, 17

Weeds can also grow on good ground.

Find good mentors and attend fellowships that are growing and believe in the power of God. The self-righteous people try make God fit in their own idealism. They become religious and make doctrines for others and justify what they do by mixing in a little word with their fear. The world (*and many of us*) has become so used to a powerless church that even the expectancy of the Pentecostal churches has decreased lower than the expectations of the early church. There are 100,000's of churches in the U.S. that have gone a year without a conversion. Many have fallen to man-made structure, carnal vision, conformity to the world and inability to include our future generations.

"For men shall be lovers of their own selves... lovers of pleasures more than lovers of God Having a form of godliness, but denying the power thereof: from such turn away." 2 Timothy 3:2-5

Many have chosen fantasy instead of truth. Fantasy is what people use when they don't want the kind of intimacy with God that requires their life. The reason we have to die to self is because if we preach any message other than God's, we can cause unfruitfulness or death. The carnal minds in this world can have churches and preach whatever they want (*homosexuality, sexually free, legalistic or religious churches*) to gain money and members, but the supernatural man will have the Kingdom building in mind, not first, but only. Our goal is to get as many as we can in the spirit of unity, because there is only one Spirit of unity.

"Knowing this, that our old man was crucified with *Him,* that the body of sin might be done away with, that we should no longer be slaves of sin. For he who has died has been freed from sin. Now if we died with Christ, we believe that we shall also live with Him" Romans 6:6-8 NKJ

"...because they received not the love of the truth, that they might be saved. And for this cause God shall send them strong delusion, that they should believe a lie: That they all might be damned who believed not the truth, but had pleasure in unrighteousness." 2 Thessalonians 2:10-12

"But seek ye first the kingdom of God, and his righteousness; and all these things shall be added unto you." Matthew 6:33

"There is one body, and one Spirit, even as ye are called in one hope of your calling; One Lord, one faith, one baptism, One God and Father of all, who is above all, and through all, and in you all." Ephesians 4:4-6

There are two kinds of religion in this world: A word that will keep you bound or a Word that will make you free. As you hear and believe at a rate that is tolerable to you, the Spirit will drop more knowledge into your being. When you are ready for a greater level, He will provide you with insight and open your eyes to receive impartation. Your meditation on the Word separates you from an ungodly lifestyle and opens up what is impossible to men, but not to God. When you close the door on your performance abilities, it opens up His most capable performances through you. With the recognition of His indwelling and external protection, we can live life without fear, worry or doubt. Our faith realizes the power available to us.

"You're hopeless, you religion scholars and Phari-sees! Frauds! You go halfway around the world to make a convert, but once you get him you make him into a replica of yourselves, double-damned." Matthew 23:15 MB

"Jesus answered and said to them, "Assuredly, I say to you, if you have faith and do not doubt, you will not only do what was done to the fig tree, but also if you say to this mountain, 'Be removed and be cast into the sea,' it will be done. And whatever things you ask in prayer, believing, you will receive." Matthew 21:21, 22 NKJ

"For God hath not given us the spirit of fear; but of power, and of love, and of a sound mind." 2 Timothy 1:7

"...whose children [namely Sarah] you become if the whole course of your life is in the doing of good, and you are not being caused to fear by even one particle of terror." 1 Peter 3:6 KW

Your born again spirit is the result of an unchanging God. When you declared Jesus Lord in your life, you find that you are no longer subject to the world's chance and probability, but the Father's protective love and guidance. God will do whatever necessary at any time and circumstance to provide for you. He becomes your first source of healing, preservation and provision. Your desire for God should be greater than performing miracles, but the desire to see the salvation and healing of more souls gives you the heart and plan of God for this life. The gifts God gives to his children are manifestations of the Spirit that are for all of us. Since the relationship with the Spirit is not just for you, you will be used to engineer transports into the kingdom.

"Every good gift and every perfect gift is from above, and comes down from the Father of lights, with whom there is no variation or shadow of turning." James 1:17 NKJ

"God is not a man, so he does not lie. He is not human, so he does not change his mind. Has he ever spoken and failed to act? Has he ever promised and not carried it through?" Numbers 23:19 NLT

"Don't bargain with God. Be direct. Ask for what you need. This is not a cat-and-mouse, hide-and-seek game we're in. If your little boy asks for a serving of fish, do you scare him with a live snake on his plate? If your little girl asks for an egg, do you trick her with a spider? As bad as you are, you wouldn't think of such a thing-you're at least decent to your own children. And don't you think the Father who conceived you in love will give the Holy Spirit when you ask him?" Luke 11:10-13 MB

"Now there are diversities of gifts, but the same Spirit. And there are differences of administrations, but the same Lord. But the manifestation of the Spirit is given to every man to profit withal." 1 Corinthians 12:4, 7

"And they that be wise shall shine as the brightness of the firmament; and they that turn many to righteousness as the stars for ever and ever." Daniel 12:3

The events in the bible are a progression of God's revelation to man. Your progress has the ability to develop in a short time. After Job ignorantly blamed God for his tragedies and was corrected by Him, he was ready to repent and walk into new faith. When you take the Word of God at face value and eliminate false doctrine you will elevate quickly.

"Behold, I am vile; what shall I answer you? I will lay my hand over my mouth." Job 40:4 NKJ

"Study to shew thyself approved unto God, a workman that needeth not to be ashamed, rightly dividing the word of truth." 2 Timothy 2:15

"But solid food belongs to those who are of full age, *that is,* those who by reason of use have their senses exercised to discern both good and evil." Hebrews 5:14 NKJ

The time is coming and is now present, that the difference between the powerful and powerless will become more evident. Preachers can have good messages, or they can have God messages. One who is sent from God, an apostle or a prophet; will correct, instruct and inspire you to change for the better. They will stir up the Holy Spirit that's already in you and ready to be revealed. There are things in you that *you don't know you know*. But God doesn't want you to be on the outside, looking in; He wants you to move inside of you and pour out from you. The secret things of God belong to His children: Mystery + God = Revelation! If the Spirit reveals it to you, you'll see it in performance and guidance. One of the mysteries of God is to find out how full of God we really are.

Get a revelation of what's in you. The anointing will work in a powerful way when your faith decides to accept the truth before the evidence is seen.

"The secret things belong unto the LORD our God: but those things which are revealed belong unto us and to our children for ever, that we may do all the words of this law." Deuteronomy 29:29

"For this cause we also, since the day we heard it, do not cease to pray for you, and to desire that ye might be filled with the knowledge of his will in all wisdom and spiritual understanding" Colossians 1:9

"This message was kept secret for centuries and generations past, but now it has been revealed to God's people. For God wanted them to know that the riches and glory of Christ are for you Gentiles, too. And this is the secret: Christ lives in you. This gives you assurance of sharing his glory." Colossians 1:26, 27 NLT

On a daily basis, God places many 'impressions' into your spirit. This river of Life continues to flow for your direction whether you pay attention to it or not. You will never be fully satisfied in life unless you follow it. With His flow, you will know you are called to *know* and won't get ahead of God and operate in the flesh. Even if the devil tried to make you look like an imposter before, the Spirit will get you into places and mentors to help you renew your mind.

The weapons of our warfare are the blood of Jesus, the Word of Jesus and the indwelling life of Jesus. When we remind ourselves that the enemy has long ago been defeated on the cross, we realize that '*name calling*' is the only thing the accuser has left. There is no opposition. We are not in a war, but a takeover. The sooner you let go of what your flesh believes, the sooner the Spirit will manifest in your life. The sooner you let go of spirit quenching friendships, the more available you will be for those who you can make a difference in their lives. Don't hang around with losers, when God called you to win. Make God your number one priority, He made you His.

If God talked to Cain, even after he committed murder (Gen 4:8-15), He will continue to talk to you. If a legion of demons got their request answered (Mark 5:12, 13), He will surely grant yours. God cherishes you. God's living Word is always speaking, but again, your faith will allow Him to talk to you. More than being a carnal or casual Christian, you are a believer, and more than a conqueror. Your name in the bible is under the *'them also which shall believe'*.

"For the weapons of our warfare are not carnal, but mighty through God to the pulling down of strong holds" 2 Corinthians 10:4

"But the Comforter, which is the Holy Ghost, whom the Father will send in my name, he shall teach you all things, and bring all things to your remembrance, whatsoever I have said unto you." John 14:26

"And from the days of John the Baptist <u>until</u> now the kingdom of heaven suffers violence..." Matthew 11:12 NKJ

"How precious also are Your thoughts to me, O God! how great is the sum of them! *If* I should count them, they are more in number than the sand: when I awake, I am still with you." Psalm 139:17, 18 NKJ

"Nay, in all these things we are more than conquerors through him that loved us."Romans 8:37

"Neither pray I for these alone, but for them also which shall believe on me through their word." John 17:23 NKJ

Out of the 600 times the New Testament mentions the Word if, it implies that there are decisions to make to confirm your calling. Only you can walk the pathway of your ordained destiny. We need to line up our thought with the written Word until it becomes a pattern of our thought life. Some examples:

"IF ye live after the flesh, ye shall die" Romans 8:13

"IF any man draw back, my soul shall have no pleasure in him." Hebrews 10:38

"IF any be a hearer of the word, and not a doer, he is like unto a man beholding his natural face in a glass" James 1:23

"IF that which ye have heard from the beginning shall remain in you, ye also shall continue in the Son, and in the Father." 1 John 2:24

"IF then you were raised with Christ, seek those things which are above, where Christ is, sitting at the right hand of God." Colossians 3:1 NKJ

"IF any man be in Christ, he is a new creature: old things are passed away; behold, all things are become new." 2 Corinthians 5:7

"IF we could control our tongues, we would be perfect and could also control ourselves in every other way." James 3:2 NLT

"**IF** any man speak, let him speak as the oracles of God;

IF If anyone ministers, *let him do it* as with the ability which God supplies." 1 Peter 4:11 NKJ

"**IF** these things be in you, and abound.. ye shall never fall" 2 Peter 1:8-10

"...**IF** our heart condemn us not, then have we confidence toward God. And whatsoever we ask, we receive of him, because we keep his commandments, and do those things that are pleasing in his sight." 1 John 3:21

The Kingdom of God is everything Jesus rules over. Learning about it will illuminate the choices that are there for you (*I cover this in another book*). The choices you make in life will help others overcome obstacles. With your faith, you will use what rightfully belongs to you. A lot of miracles in the Word were first time events. You can even be the first to have an original miracle that no one has even seen before. We should want God to operate in ways that we've never seen! We can pursue the miraculous because of the righteous One within us. We have the greatest covenant ever available to us with Christ our King as our mediator and can have the best;

"But now He has obtained a more excellent ministry, inasmuch as He is also Mediator of a better covenant, which was established on better promises." Hebrews 8:6 NKJ

"I can do all things through Christ which strengthens me." Philippians 4:13 NKJ

"But earnestly desire the best gifts." 1 Corinthians 12:31 NKJ

We may start off slow at first, praying for at headaches or recent occurrences where the enemy attempts to recruit someone into accepting something from a spirit of pain or infirmity. Even laying on hands and believing God for that is a good super natural start. The world comes out with new diseases frequently and would like to recruit you into believing what they say instead of God's report. Our choice of believing God's report or man's report; The Spirit's report or someone who *tried it and it didn't work*, or someone who *wasn't sure when they asked*, and told you it didn't work?

"Who has believed our report? And to whom is the arm of the LORD revealed?" Isaiah 53:1 NKJ

"If you don't know what you're doing, pray to the Father. He loves to help. You'll get his help, and won't be condescended to when you ask for it. Ask boldly, believingly, without a second thought. People who 'worry their prayers' are like wind whipped waves. Don't think you're going to get anything from the Master that way, adrift at sea, keeping your options open." James 1:5-8 MB

In the natural, we have the choice to take a life or make a life. We have so much more in the spiritual, because we are spiritual beings. We have been given authority to interrupt the world system of suffering and change it. If you don't like the circumstances, don't let it stay buried in death but pray for life to come into the unrighteous situations for the joy of all.

"Heal the sick, cleanse the lepers, raise the dead, cast out devils: freely ye have received, freely give." Matthew 10:8

"...Most assuredly, I say to you, whatever you ask the Father in My name He will give you. Until now you have

asked nothing in My name. Ask, and you will receive, that your joy may be full." John 16:23, 24 NKJ

When we are willing, we are called. When we are obedient, we are chosen. When the Lord chooses you, He will make sure the Kingdom is personally taught to you in abundance.

"For many are called, but few are chosen." Matthew 22:14

"You did not choose Me, but I chose you and appointed you that you should go and bear fruit, and *that* your fruit should remain, that whatever you ask the Father in My name He may give you." John 15:16 NKJ

"Wherefore the rather, brethren, give diligence to make your calling and election sure: for if ye do these things, ye shall never fall: For so an entrance shall be ministered unto you abundantly into the everlasting kingdom of our Lord and Saviour Jesus Christ." 2 Peter 1:10, 11

CHAPTER 4

The God Kind of Man

"As Jesus is, so are we in the world" 1 John 4:17

Y ou are not only a man or woman of God, but you are a man or woman with God *in* you. Man was made in His image and likeness. It is the plan of God for you to be like Him and have the God kind of faith and have dominion. You will experience your life according to your perception of yourself with God indwelling in you and what perception you have of God. If you think God is all powerful (*and He is*) and you don't have to do anything but accept your '*get out of hell free card*' and '*wait on the Lord*' think again. God doesn't control everything, but He gave us the power and authority to observe and teach His commandments over all the earth. It is up to us to let Him not only be God, but also Lord. Many may wait for a move of God, but God is waiting for us to move and get a revelation of the plan He's already given us. If you think that He gave you power (*and He did*) you will realize that He wants to use you to do greater works.

"Then God said, "Let Us make man in Our image, according to Our likeness; let <u>them</u> have dominion over the fish of the sea, over the birds of the air, and over the

cattle, over all the earth and over every creeping thing that creeps on the earth." Genesis 1:26, 27 NKJ

"You have put all things in subjection under his feet. For in that he put all in subjection under him, he left nothing that is not put under him... " Hebrews 2:8

The Lord's plan never changes, although angels and men have made their own unsuccessful plans with many believing in them. The plan for us to have dominion was God's idea. Jesus came to show us what it would be like to have the Spirit upon us and experience that dominion with consistency. Although many Old Testament prophets would do great exploits, we could see their faults. With Jesus, we could see more of the potential of men with the indwelling of His Holy Spirit. We could see the possibilities of victory on every side and great assurance in the way things really are. He walked on water, stopped winds and displayed dominion as men were called to do. He wouldn't ask the disciples to look for their faith or feed the multitude without knowing that the power is already available in them.

"God forbid: yea, let God be true, but every man a liar..." Romans 3:4

"And they came to him, and awoke him, saying, Master, master, we perish. Then he arose, and rebuked the wind and the raging of the water: and they ceased, and there was a calm. And he said unto them, Where is your faith?..." Luke 8:24, 25

"And when it was evening, his disciples came to him, saying, This is a desert place, and the time is now past; send the multitude away, that they may go into the villages, and buy themselves victuals. But Jesus said

unto them, They need not depart; <u>give ye them</u> to eat."
Matthew 14:15, 16

The things He did as a man were things we could do
as men. He is the master and we are his disciples. We are
to be like our master. We are to be like He is. It is similar
to Jacob's son Joseph, who had the highest position in his
surroundings and was a mouthpiece for his master;

"Then the seventy returned with joy, saying, "Lord, even
the demons are subject to us in Your name." And He said
to them, "I saw Satan fall like lightning from heaven.
Behold, I give you the authority to trample on serpents
and scorpions, and over all the power of the enemy, and
nothing shall by any means hurt you. Nevertheless do
not rejoice in this, that the spirits are subject to you, but
rather rejoice because your names are written in heaven."
Luke 10:17-20 NKJ

"It is enough for the disciple that he be as his master, and
the servant as his lord..." Matthew 10:25

"Who then is a faithful and wise servant, whom his lord
hath made ruler over his household, to give them meat in
due season?" Matthew 24:45

"Herein is our love made perfect...because as he is, so
are we in this world." 1 John 4:17

"You shall be over my house, and all my people shall
be ruled according to your word; only in regard to the
throne will I be greater than you." Genesis 41:40 NKJ

Jesus came on the battlefield being tempted by Satan and
proved that for every temptation there's a way to escape and

be without sin (1 Cor 10:13). He let others know that there was choice and grace available for them to do the same, even if we have missed the mark before;

"...Don't return to a sinning life or something worse might happen." John 5:14 MB

"...Go on your way. From now on, don't sin." John 8:11 MB

It was only right for Jesus to be like us, so he could experientially relate to us.

"But we see Jesus, who was made a little lower than the angels, for the suffering of death crowned with glory and honor, that He, by the grace of God, might taste death for everyone... For both He who sanctifies and those who are being sanctified *are* all of one, for which reason He is not ashamed to call them brethren... Inasmuch then as the children have partaken of flesh and blood, He Himself likewise shared in the same, that through death He might destroy him who had the power of death, that is, the devil, and release those who through fear of death were all their lifetime subject to bondage. For indeed He does not give aid to angels, but He does give aid to the seed of Abraham. Therefore, in all things He had to be made like *His* brethren, that He might be a merciful and faithful High Priest in things *pertaining* to God, to make propitiation for the sins of the people. For in that He Himself has suffered, being tempted, He is able to aid those who are tempted. Hebrews 2:9-18 NKJ

The meditation of Jesus came out in His words. The Light of the world also proclaimed *we* are the light of the world (Matt 5:14). When we get a true revelation of our heavenly identity, our inner meditation of who we are in Christ will keep us from missing the mark and fulfilling our destiny. The 'I am' is in you. Your intentionally given nature is like the 'I am'. Whether you forget or not, or people tell you different, the bible says you are a new born again creation.

"I am the vine, ye are the branches..." John 15:5

"... I am the light of the world." John 9:5

"I am the resurrection, and the life..." John 11:25

"I am come to send fire on the earth..." Luke 12:49

"And all Mine are Yours, and Yours are Mine, and I am glorified in them." John 17:10 NKJ

"Therefore, if anyone *is* in Christ, *he is* a new creation; old things have passed away; behold, all things have become new." 2 Corinthians 5:17 NKJ

We must establish ourselves as a God man. Whether male, female, Jew or adopted outsider, we are one in Christ. In order to be a good leader, you have to be a good follower. Stephan's reputation grew from the business of helping people to great miracles. After he took care of physical needs with love, he took care of spiritual needs with power. We need to do well with the gifts God gives us grace to have, and He will make us faithful over more. We grow and mature and watch our gifts make room for us.

"There is neither Jew nor Greek, there is neither bond nor free, there is neither male nor female: for ye are all one in Christ Jesus." Galatians 3:28

"Wherefore, brethren, look ye out among you seven men of honest report, full of the Holy Ghost and wisdom, whom we may appoint over this business. But we will give ourselves continually to prayer, and to the ministry of the word. And the saying pleased the whole multitude: and they chose Stephen, a man full of faith and of the Holy Ghost... Whom they set before the apostles: and when they had prayed, they laid their hands on them." Acts 6:3-6

"And Stephen, full of faith and power, did great wonders and miracles among the people." Acts 6:8

"As each one has received a gift, minister it to one another, as good stewards of the manifold grace of God. If anyone speaks, *let him speak* as the oracles of God. If anyone ministers, *let him do it* as with the ability which God supplies, that in all things God may be glorified..." 1 Peter 4:10, 11 NKJ

"His master commended him: 'Good work! You did your job well. From now on be my partner...'" Matthew 25:23 MB

"A man's gift makes room for him, and brings him before great men." Proverbs 18:16 NKJ

Jesus Himself learned obedience *experientially* in human form. It wasn't that He learned how to be obedient, but came in life as a follower (*of chosen leaders*) until the Spirit of the Lord came upon Him to do great works. He didn't talk about His deity, but the anointing. People placed a demand on the anointing of Jesus. Like Jesus, we cannot just go to a hospital and heal everyone just because we want to. His teaching and preaching had to be different than others with no power. His reputation built over time and the big and little things He did allowed the expectancy of people to come to Him with greater faith. The talk of each city spread His reputation and planted seeds of hope and faith. Although the humanistic ways of people wanted to promote Him and make Him king, His humbleness and desire was not to make a reputation for Himself, but to reveal the power available in men in His earthly time and the power that was to come after His resurrection.

"Though he was God's Son, he learned trusting-obedience by what he suffered, just as we do." Hebrews 5:8 MB

"The Spirit of the LORD is upon Me, Because He has anointed Me To preach the gospel to the poor; He has sent Me to heal the brokenhearted, To proclaim liberty to the captives And recovery of sight to the blind, To set at liberty those who are oppressed; To proclaim the acceptable year of the LORD." Luke 4:18, 19 NKJ

"When Jesus therefore perceived that they would come and take him by force, to make him a king, he departed again into a mountain himself alone." John 6:15

"But when Jesus knew *it*, He withdrew from there. And great multitudes followed Him, and He healed them all. Yet He warned them not to make Him known" Matthew 12:15, 16 NKJ

Jesus built a reputation of his character. His words would captivate even those who tried to arrest Him. His conversations drew disciples to Himself even before His first miracle. When Jesus performed the miracle at Cana His reputation was spread by the servants and had to spark a lot of conversations, stories and renewed faith. When He came back to

Cana, the crowd was ready with expectation. When He cast the legion of demons out in Nazarene, the same people who begged Him to get out of their town did not meditate on the loss of their pigs, but on the potential of His power. The young man was left to spread His reputation there. When He came back across the water, the bible reports that everyone in the town who touched Him received healing. The disciples who trusted in Him would also go ahead into towns and prepare the people for a demonstration of God's power. Through much resistance and opposition, His gifts made room for Him.

"...No man ever spoke like this Man" John 7:46 NKJ

"On the third day there was a wedding in Cana of Galilee, and the mother of Jesus was there. Now both Jesus and His disciples were invited to the wedding... When the master of the feast had tasted the water that was made wine, and did not know where it came from (but the servants who had drawn the water knew... This beginning of signs Jesus did in Cana of Galilee, and manifested His glory; and His disciples believed in Him." John 2:1, 2, 9, 11 NKJ

"Jesus came again into Cana of Galilee, where he made the water wine. And there was a certain nobleman, whose son was sick at Capernaum. When he heard that Jesus had come out of Judaea into Galilee, he went to him, and implored Him to come down and heal his son, for he was at the point of death. Then Jesus said to him... "Go thy way; your son lives!" So the man believed the word that Jesus spoke to him, and he went his way. And as he was now going down, his servants met him, and told him, saying, "Your son lives" And himself believed, and his whole house." John 4:46-53 MB

"And they came over unto the other side of the sea, to the country of the Gadarenes. And when he was come out of the boat, immediately there met him out of the tombs a man with an unclean spirit, who had his dwelling among the tombs; and no man could bind him, no, not with chains... So all the demons begged Him, saying, Send us into the swine, that we may enter into them. And at once Jesus gave them permission. Then the unclean spirits went out, and entered into the swine...So those that fed the swine fled, and told it in the city, and in the country... And they come to Jesus, and saw the one *who had been* demon-possessed, and had the legion, sitting, and clothed, and in his right mind. And they were afraid... Then they began to plead with him to depart from their region. And when he had got into the boat, he that had been demon-possessed begged Him that he might be with him. However Jesus did not permit him, "Go home to your friends, and tell them what great things the Lord has done for you, and how he has had compassion on you." And he departed, and began to proclaim in Decapolis all that Jesus had done for him; and all marveled."Mark 5:1-20

"And when Jesus was passed over again by ship unto the other side, much people gathered unto him: and he was nigh unto the sea." Mark 5:21

"When they had crossed over, they came to the land of Gennesaret and anchored there. And when they came out of the boat, immediately the people recognized Him, ran through that whole surrounding region, and began to carry about on beds those who were sick to wherever they heard He was. Wherever He entered, into villages, cities, or the country, they laid the sick in the market-places, and begged Him that they might just touch the

hem of His garment. And as many as touched Him were made well." Mark 6:53-56 NKJ

The pattern Jesus used for teaching, preaching and healing works well. Any born-again believer who decides to choose to be chosen by God and acts upon the words of Jesus to teach will have the Spirit of the Lord upon them to do greater works. God will not force any choice upon us, but we can choose mediocrity or allow power in our life because of the Holy Spirit that has been given. Not only will goodness and mercy follow you, but signs and wonders accompany those who desire to penetrate the earth with the finger of God. As we develop our relationship with God, we will know who to lay hands on and who not to. We learn when to wait until a person is ready to receive and not to lay hands on any man suddenly. We don't try to '*do*' the kingdom, but follow the Spirit's leading. We don't want to become performance orientated in works, but have compassion on people and teach them how to receive. When we've grown up past asking God for so much when He's already promised us all good things pertaining to life, we began to intercede on the behalf of others.

"And He said to them, "Go into all the world and preach the gospel to every creature. He who believes and is baptized will be saved; but he who does not believe will be condemned. And these signs will follow those who believe: In My name they will cast out demons; they will speak with new tongues; they will take up serpents; and if they drink anything deadly, it will by no means hurt them; they will lay hands on the sick, and they will recover." Mark 16:15-18 NKJ

"Do not lay hands on anyone hastily, nor share in other people's sins; keep yourself pure." 1 Timothy 5:22 NKJ

Ever since the fall of Adam, God has always tried to get us to speak. As men fell into the slavery of condemnation, it seemed so unreal to be able to speak to things. They began to fear and have an expectation of evil and control instead of the God given peace and liberty. When God called Moses to be a leader, he made excuses to the Lord. He had identity crises;

"And Moses said unto God, Who am I, that I should go unto Pharaoh, and that I should bring forth the children of Israel out of Egypt?" Exodus 3:11

"Then Moses answered and said, 'But suppose they will not believe me or listen to my voice; suppose they say, 'The LORD has not appeared to you.'" So the LORD said to him, "What *is* that in your hand?" he said, A rod." Exodus 4:1, 2 NKJ

"Then Moses said to the LORD, 'O my Lord, I *am* not eloquent, neither before nor since you have spoken to your servant; but I *am* slow of speech and slow of tongue.'" Exodus 4:10 NKJ

For so many years, God expressed power through man with only a stick. Moses used his rod to part the sea, to fight battles and get water out of a rock for the children of Israel (Ex. 14:16, 17:5, 6-9). Men did not live up to their potential. In the Numbers 20:8, when the children of Israel were thirsty again, God told Moses to *speak* to the rock. Moses spoke to the people and used his rod again to *beat* the rock. For this, he could not make it to the 'promised land' with his people (Num 20:10-12). If Moses spoke to the rock without touching it, mankind could have had such a breakthrough an example of the power of words.

"Now therefore, go, and I will be with your mouth and teach you what you shall say." Exodus 4:12 NKJ

Even now that we have recorded Jesus in history telling us to speak to circumstances, many still have a hard time getting a hold of this principle. At least we have gotten the basic 'confess with our mouth the Lord Jesus' to be powerfully saved (Rom 10:9), but it doesn't stop there. Most of the New Testament scriptures don't refer to heaven but to our life on earth and the way that devils and doctrines attempt to weaken and hinder the Word in our lives. The Word sanctifies us from the world making us holy, or set apart from the world;

"As obedient children, not conforming yourselves to the former lusts, *as* in your ignorance; but as He who called you *is* holy, you also be holy in all *your* conduct, because it is written, Because it is written, Be ye holy; for I am holy." 1 Peter 1:14-16 NKJ

The bible is a revelation of who we are in God. It tells us how to talk to God and how to talk to circumstances of the world and gives examples of both. Jesus talks about two forms of voice orientated power. The first: speaking to things, and the second: praying;

"So Jesus answered and said to them, "Have faith in God. For assuredly, I say to you, whoever says to this mountain, 'Be removed and be cast into the sea,' and does not doubt in his heart, but believes that those things he says will be done, he will have whatever he says. Therefore I say to you, whatever things you ask when you pray, believe that you receive *them,* and you will have *them.*" Mark 11:22-24 NKJ

"For everyone who asks receives, and he who seeks finds, and to him who knocks it will be opened." Luke 11:10 NKJ

Because our names are written in heaven, we have the kingdom rule within us. Your supernatural rule is based upon your acceptance of kingship from believing and receiving. It is not far away, but the indwelling powers of words are within you. When we perceive ourselves to be true men *of* God, the Conqueror rises within us.

"See what I've given you? Safe passage as you walk on snakes and scorpions, and protection from every assault of the Enemy. No one can put a hand on you. All the same, the great triumph is not in your authority over evil, but in God's authority over you and presence with you. Not what you do for God but what God does for you-that's the agenda for rejoicing." Luke 10:19, 20 MB

"But what does it say? *"The word is near you, in your mouth and in your heart"* (that is, the word of faith which we preach)" Romans 10:8 NKJ

"...in all these things we are more than conquerors through him that loved us." Romans 8:37

When you were saved, your spirit man took on the nature of God and became a new creation. You were called to be a believer. Jesus never said this power is for me, but not for you. You can let God live in you, or let the old man live. The inner direction is available to put impossibilities to shame and take limits off of your life. It helps those needing the revelation of your personal God indwelling. Promotion comes because you know what God has promised and you believe it. You have the potential to be all or nothing with

God. Let the Word elevate you so that God can be seen. If the angels are camped around those who God loves, will we just let them sit on an *'unemployment line'* or get them involved with our bold speaking? If He could have called a legion of angels, we can surely call for God's help in need. When you show up, God's nature is there.

"And he said, The things which are impossible with men are possible with God." Luke 18:27

"For he shall give his angels charge over you, to keep you in all thy ways." Psalm 91:11 NKJ

"Or do you think that I cannot now pray to My Father, and He will provide Me with more than twelve legions of angels?" Matthew 26:53 NKJ

"God is a safe place to hide, ready to help when we need him." Psalm 46:1 MB

God wants the cooperation of our speech. If life, our words are perhaps 2% what we say and 98% how we say it. When words are wrapped with faith, confidence, love and compassion of God, His power reaches out through us to plant seeds, intercede and speak miracles into place. When things are greater than our mental ability to grasp, the Spirit will take over for us. The Spirit will replace good intentions with *God intentions*. When we began to speak in an unknown tongue we strengthen ourselves and speak powerful mysteries. Sometimes if we knew the incredible things we were saying, we would doubt it. To pray for the gift of interpreting would release the revelation of what is being spoken when we are able to be faithful lover much;

"God's Spirit is right alongside helping us along. If we don't know how or what to pray, it doesn't matter. He does our praying in and for us, making prayer out of our wordless sighs, our aching groans. He knows us far better than we know ourselves." Romans 8:26, 27 MB

"A person who speaks in tongues is strengthened personally." 1 Corinthians 14:4 NLT

"For he who speaks in a tongue does not speak to men but to God, for no one understands *him;* however, in the spirit he speaks mysteries." 1 Corinthians 14:2 NKJ

"Therefore let him who speaks in a tongue pray that he may interpret." 1 Corinthians 14:13 NKJ

"So, when you pray in your private prayer language, don't hoard the experience for yourself. Pray for the insight and ability to bring others into that intimacy" 1 Corinthians 14:13 MB

"...'Well *done,* good and faithful servant; you were faithful over a few things, I will make you ruler over many things. Enter into the joy of your lord." Matthew 25:21 NKJ

We have established some good ground on using the same anointing that Jesus had, and powerful words that are waiting to flow out of your inner being. The purpose for the anointing is to reveal that God is truly in us and lead others to worship Him. The power is not to glorify us, but God;

"...the words that I speak unto you, they are spirit, and they are life." John 6:63

"He who believes in Me, as the Scripture has said, out of his heart will flow rivers of living water." John 7:38 NKJ

"And thus are the secrets of his heart made manifest; and so falling down on his face he will worship God, and report that God is in you of a truth." 1 Corinthians 14:25

"But have renounced the hidden things of dishonesty, not walking in craftiness, nor handling the word of God deceitfully; but by manifestation of the truth commending ourselves to every man's conscience in the sight of God." 2 Corinthians 4:2

God is in you. Not just a part of Him, but His fullness. He doesn't have a size, the same as our spirit does not have one. We are called to be channels of heaven for people to tune into. When we represent the Spirit of God in transparency, anyone who desires to should be able to connect to Him through us.

"And I am sure that, when I come unto you, I shall come in the fulness of the blessing of the gospel of Christ." Romans 15:29

"to know the love of Christ which passes knowledge; that you may be filled with all the fullness of God." Ephesians 3:19 NKJ

The resident power of the Lord must be anticipated, expected and invited to set the stage for the anointing. This will create an atmosphere for healing and miracles. When we live the word, we are convincing when we preach. When we have an 'inside the veil' experience, people will notice our anointing. A blind man must know beyond the shadow of a doubt, that you have the anointing to heal him. People must see it in your eyes *that you know*, that you know. People must see in your lifestyle, the super natural partnership that you have with God to make a solid connection.

As you develop your relationship with God, discernment comes super-naturally. When you abide in the shadow of the Almighty, and stand in His presence, your spiritual eyes open. You will also be like Jesus and see the faith in others;

"For as he thinks in his heart, so is he..." Proverbs 23:7 NKJ

"But Jesus perceived their wickedness..." Matthew 22:18

"*This* man heard Paul speaking. Paul, observing him intently and seeing that he had faith to be healed" Acts 14:9 NKJ

Even now you can feel the heart of God to testify to you and look for opportunities to bring others into the kingdom and glory. But before your shadows start healing, people need to know where you've been, and who you've spent time with. This comes out in your words of Spirit influenced power. Then, instead of giving alms to the beggar, it will be easier to heal him. You'll tell him to rise up and walk. You'll be a living witness that God can use people like He did with the apostles. Your faith will have no respect of opinions, limits, time, distance or circumstances. There will be no intimidation. Jesus talked and people got healed. People came to Him because of His reputation.

"Let this mind be in you, which was also in Christ Jesus" Philippians 2:5

"And he took him by the right hand and lifted *him* up, and immediately his feet and ankle bones received strength. So he, leaping up, stood and walked and entered the temple with them—walking, leaping, and praising God. And all the people saw him walking and praising God." Acts 3:7-9 NKJ

People are waiting on God. They've heard the stories. They wait for motivated declarers of the Word. Will you take the call, or think for yourself and to yourself? If you do take the call, you are chosen to be the God kind of man. When you hear someone needing healing, you won't use sympathy, but power and ask; "Can I pray for you?" God is not moved by our needs, but His Son has done the work and waits for the Seed that has been planted within us to be watered by His Spirit. Those of us who are in Christ, we have been given the nature and character of Jesus to do greater works.

"As His divine power has given to us all things that *pertain* to life and godliness, through the knowledge of Him who called us by glory and virtue, by which have been given to us exceedingly great and precious promises, that through these you may be partakers of the divine nature, having escaped the corruption *that is* in the world through lust." 2 Peter 1:3, 4 NKJ

Put your self esteem in the same manner God has validated you in. God's validation will empower you to His incarnate, quickening residence in you. The old man in you has died and been crucified, don't let him be raised up by the world. You are not here to accept the world's reports or opinions. You can think like God, or you can think like a regular man. The Holy Spirit has enlarged the physical territory of God by multiplying his guidance and rulership in us. When you speak to somebody, think about some things you would want that person to say about you after you leave. Let it be more powerful as you walk your brief time here on earth.

"No soldier when in service gets entangled in the enter-prises of [civilian] life; his aim is to satisfy and please the one who enlisted him." 2 Timothy 2:4 AMP

"As Jesus is, so are we in the world" 1 John 4:17

God is interested in us to renew our mind. We need to reflect the image of God to prove the existence of the resurrection of Jesus, by allowing Him to live in our lives. The way we do that is to renew our mind with the word and make our bodies a living sacrifice (*He would not ask us to do anything He didn't do*). We let the '*old man*' die and let the new man live. We are bought with a price and the Lord wants a return on His investment. We should let Him own all of us. His intention is for the body is for it to be well. He takes care of His body. He is more interested in it than we have a tendency to be.

"So here's what I want you to do, God helping you: Take your everyday, ordinary life your sleeping, eating, going-to-work, and walking-around life and place it before God as an offering. Embracing what God does for you is the best thing you can do for him. Don't become so well-adjusted to your culture that you fit into it without even thinking. Instead, fix your attention on God. You'll be changed from the inside out. Readily recognize what he wants from you, and quickly respond to it. Unlike the culture around you, always dragging you down to its level of immaturity, God brings the best out of you, develops well-formed maturity in you." Romans 12:1, 2 MB

"Since, then, we do not have the excuse of ignorance, everything—and I do mean everything—connected with that old way of life has to go. It's rotten through and through. Get rid of it! And then take on an entirely new way of life—a God-fashioned life, a life renewed from the inside and working itself into your conduct as God accurately reproduces his character in you. What this adds up to, then, is this." Ephesians 4:22-24 MB

"What? know ye not that your body is the temple of the Holy Ghost which is in you, which ye have of God, and ye are not your own? For ye are bought with a price: therefore glorify God in your body, and in your spirit, which are God's." 1 Corinthians 6:19, 20

"For no one ever hated his own flesh, but nourishes and cherishes it, just as the Lord *does* the church" Ephesians 5:29 NKJ

God made us like Jesus in our spirit man, the rest is up to us. We should not want to pray *'Lord, make me like Jesus'* to make ourselves feel better by leaving the work up to Him. We need to purify our own soul by making good decisions about the company we keep, the music we choose to listen to and the preaching we attend. We can have our senses exercised to a point where the devil's thoughts scream before they get to us.

"...Cleanse your hands, ye sinners; and purify your hearts, ye double minded." James 4:8

"I wrote unto you in an epistle not to company with fornicators" 1 Corinthians 5:9

"As the end approaches, people are going to be self-absorbed, money-hungry, self-promoting, stuck-up, profane, contemptuous of parents, crude, coarse, dog-eat-dog, unbending, slanderers, impulsively wild, savage, cynical, treacherous, ruthless, bloated windbags, addicted to lust, and allergic to God. They'll make a show of religion, but behind the scenes they're animals. Stay clear of these people" 2 Timothy 3:2-5 MB

"Don't lazily slip back into those old grooves of evil, doing just what you feel like doing. You didn't know any better then; you do now. As obedient children, let yourselves be pulled into a way of life shaped by God's life, a life energetic and blazing with holiness. God said, "I am holy; you be holy."" 1 Peter 1:13-16 MB

When you do not renew your mind to God, you become a compromiser by nature. You go back to default settings by sleeping, eating or entertainment, things that become second nature to us. But God should be your first nature. There's no third party, just blessing or cursing that comes to what spiritual influence we are willing to fill our minds and actions with. You cannot be just a hearer of the word, but your transformation comes from being a doer of the word. In the natural, if we continued to drive around in circles, we would get a map. In the spiritual, we have a God to ask for direction and we should never listen to a second opinion. When your mind is in the singleness of God, you receive freely from the Lord.

"If any of you lacks wisdom, let him ask of God, who gives to all liberally and without reproach, and it will be given to him. But let him ask in faith, with no doubting, for he who doubts is like a wave of the sea driven and tossed by the wind. For let not that man suppose that he will receive anything from the Lord; *he is* a double-minded man, unstable in all his ways." James 1:5-8 NKJ

"But be doers of the word, and not hearers only, deceiving yourselves. For if anyone is a hearer of the word and not a doer, he is like a man observing his natural face in a mirror; for he observes himself, goes away, and immediately forgets what kind of man he was." James 1:22-24 NKJ

We receive a nature and character of Jesus to do greater works. Once you have dealt with the yoke in your life, then you be better prepared to deal with the yoke in others. The spiritual influence has the biggest effect with our natural bodies. In this way God can use you mightily and do things without you even knowing. In the fight of faith we don't fight people, but the fight is against the demonic influence in them that will try to get you away from your call, so we only speak to them in the position of victory. The adversary is known for having you think something and making you believe it was your thought. The quickest way to have victory over him is to do exactly the opposite of what he tells you. If he cannot get you to think on your own, he'll try to get someone else to help you think his way. He'll try to fight you the most when your miracle is being delivered. If your character is under attack by depression, fear or worry, you must immediately get some spiritual food.

"Wipe that ugly sneer off your own face, and you might be fit to offer a washcloth to your neighbor." Matthew 7:5 MB

"We use our powerful God-tools for smashing warped philosophies, tearing down barriers erected against the truth of God, fitting every loose thought and emotion and impulse into the structure of life shaped by Christ. Our tools are ready at hand for clearing the ground of every obstruction and building lives of obedience into maturity." 2 Corinthians 10:5, 6 MB

"For we wrestle not against flesh and blood, but against principalities, against powers, against the rulers of the darkness of this world, against spiritual wickedness in high places." Ephesians 6:12

"Lest Satan should get an advantage of us: for we are not ignorant of his devices." 2 Corinthians 2:11

We can boldly confess our possession of a supernatural ability. As Jesus went around healing all that were oppressed by the devil, you are on the pathway to do the same. God didn't make a mistake when He called you. Through all of us, Jesus is doing more now than He ever did. You will always have supernatural help. Demons tremble at the thought of what will happen when we get the revelation of who we are and who is in us. When we believe, receive and stand on His promise, our constant approval of Him will bring strength and revelation to our life, and the life of the spirit world.

"Through faith also Sara herself received strength to conceive seed, and was delivered of a child when she was past age, because she judged him faithful who had promised." Hebrews 11:11

Jesus did things strategically. When Jesus told the man who was possessed with the Legion, He knew the man would be a better 'evangelist' to get other people ready for their miracle, then to come and be a disciple. Ask the Lord for wisdom in choosing the people you spend time with. Learn the strategic thinking of what will happen in future events (*like chess or billiards*) to give you the bigger picture. With eternity in mind, you'll always have the God kind of view. Exercise your faith by talking to people with hope, faith and eternity in mind. Learn to perceive by setting your priorities continuously on the plan of God. Let your strategy be in the flow of the living Word.

"As Jesus was getting into the boat, the demon-delivered man begged to go along, but he wouldn't let him. Jesus said, "Go home to your own people. Tell them your story—what the Master did, how he had mercy on you." The man went back and began to preach in the Ten Towns area about what Jesus had done for him. He was the talk of the town." Mark 5:18-20 MB

"Tell us, therefore, what do You think? Is it lawful to pay taxes to Caesar, or not? But Jesus perceived their wickedness..." Matthew 22:17, 18 NKJ

"And there sat a certain man at Lystra, impotent in his feet, being a cripple from his mother's womb, who never had walked: The same heard Paul speak: who stedfastly beholding him, and <u>perceiving</u> that he had faith to be healed..." Acts 14:8, 9

When we know that our unchanging Father has always desired us to reign with His Spirit, we can put things in proper perspective. Perspective puts you into a place where you haven't arrived yet. Perspective makes you realize that out of your mouth comes the successful and mighty Sword of God. Christ destroyed the opposing power and now you are around to destroy the works of the devil through confession, prayer, preaching and lifestyle. We must see a vision of Christ, the One we should be like, and be around people who share our eternal vision and feed us the word and stay in an agreement in the lines that the enemy cannot cross.

"Brethren, I count not myself to have apprehended: but this one thing I do, forgetting those things which are behind, and reaching forth unto those things which are before, I press toward the mark for the prize of the high calling of God in Christ Jesus." Philippians 3:13, 14

"And take the helmet of salvation, and the sword of the Spirit, which is the word of God" Ephesians 6:17

"For the word of God is quick, and powerful, and sharper than any twoedged sword, piercing even to the dividing asunder of soul and spirit, and of the joints and marrow, and is a discerner of the thoughts and intents of the heart." Hebrews 4:12

We need to be ready to be used by the resident power from within us. With the Spirit we can lead cities and nations with the potential of provision, power and peace in God's will. There is no limit to an anointing of power and strength we can find in Him when necessary for kingdom building. We've even seen the same in Old Testament times. If God is the limit, there is no ceiling of good works. To be able to make water into taste and color, the potential to make stones into bread and defying weather conditions were things that Jesus did as a man and not God, even as Peter walked on the water himself.

Your boldness will have greater angels showing up when you go to another level. Demonic spirits will shake at the Presence of God in you. If Jesus could have confidence with His touch, realize that He would like to touch people through you.

"And when Jesus was come into Peter's house, he saw his wife's mother laid, and sick of a fever. And he touched her hand, and the fever left her: and she arose, and ministered unto them." Matthew 8:14, 15

CHAPTER 5

Stumbling Blocks

The enemy has made stumbling blocks for the body of Christ for a long time. In an effort to stall for time on a sure judgment, he has made plans to hinder the knowledge of available power and has stunted the growth of many Christians. Faith in the world system of unbelief also comes by hearing and people are being dominated by what they consider. We will all experience our lives according to our perception of God. A shortage of knowledge is prevention to full intimacy with Him. Many times a person keeps the built up stumbling blocks of generations past by not studying and relying on opinions instead of the Word. How many people in church have not read the whole New Testament? How many have read and not believed? How many have thought God is in control of everything and we have nothing to do with what happens here? How many have thought God should work like a '*magic wand*', or that healing should be done *their way* or have a *formula* that should work each time? They've tried to pray and when they didn't see or feel immediate results; they held on to the experience of the circumstances and mentally threw away the truth, instead of holding on to the Truth and not accepting the circumstances. This is as if their way of thinking was more correct than God. It is much more rational to expect God to keep His promises than to break them. God's own people have suffered and their ignorance has caused generations to suffer. Through spiritual education, the body of Christ will rise up and be mighty on the earth. We will use the Word of God to fight against the '*land mines*' the enemy has set up for us.

"whose minds the god of this age has blinded, who do not believe, lest the light of the gospel of the glory of Christ, who is the image of God, should shine on them." 2 Corinthians 4:4 NKJ

"For I say, through the grace given unto me, to every man that is among you, not to think of himself more highly than he ought to think..." Romans 12:3

"My people are destroyed for lack of knowledge..." Hosea 4:6

"For we wrestle not against flesh and blood, but against principalities, against powers, against the rulers of the darkness of this world, against spiritual wickedness in high places." Ephesians 6:12

Having two opinions in the mind about the word will make you unstable and subject to the philosophy of men who invite others to their worldly speculation. If doubt, fear or unbelief is added unto the truth you have received, the truth is diluted. We cannot pray '*If it be your will*' and not know what to expect. We must know that it is God's will to heal us. We are to take heed to His Word by thinking in faith, speaking in faith and living in faith. He reveals His name and nature way back in the book of Exodus;

"But let him ask in faith, with no doubting, for he who doubts is like a wave of the sea driven and tossed by the wind. For let not that man suppose that he will receive anything from the Lord; *he is* a double-minded man, unstable in all his ways." James 1:6-8 NKJ

"No man can serve two masters: for either he will hate the one, and love the other; or else he will hold to the one, and despise the other..." Matthew 6:24

"As ye have therefore received Christ Jesus the Lord, so walk ye in him: Rooted and built up in him, and stablished in the faith, as ye have been taught, abounding therein with thanksgiving. Beware lest any man spoil you through philosophy and vain deceit, after the tradition of men, after the rudiments of the world, and not after Christ." Colossians 2:6-8

"Who his own self bare our sins in his own body on the tree, that we, being dead to sins, should live unto righteousness: by whose stripes ye were healed." 1 Peter 2:24

"... for I am the LORD who heals you." Exodus 15:26 NKJ

We are instructed to teach ourselves and those around us the truths or commandments of God. For those who have not known the availability to get close, or 'draw near' to the mind of God, they stumble on what His will is. Many people have been going to church for decades and still stumble on receiving from God's word. You may hear people say *'God moves in mysterious ways"* or quote the sayings of Isaiah before the Holy Spirit was given; *'His thoughts are not our thoughts' or 'Eyes have not seen ,nor have ears heard'* This may make someone think that God won't reveal things to you. God is not mysterious to His children, but gives us knowledge by revelation.

"Go therefore, and make disciples... Teaching them to observe all things that I have commanded you..." Matthew 28, 19, 20 NKJ

"That is what the Scriptures mean when they say, "No eye has seen, no ear has heard, and no mind has imagined what God has prepared for those who love him." But it was to us that God revealed these things by his Spirit. For his Spirit searches out everything and shows us God's deep secrets." 1 Corinthians 2:9, 10 NLT

"Now we have received, not the spirit of the world, but the spirit which is of God; that we might know the things that are freely given to us of God." 1 Corinthians 2:12

"For this cause we... pray for you, and to desire that ye might be filled with the knowledge of his will in all wisdom and spiritual understanding" Colossians 1:9

Some things may be revealed by pastors who bring great messages on the power of God in the church, but other members and leaders will intentionally divide and disrupt or ignorantly contradict what is coming from the pulpit in smaller meetings or *'parking lot'* messages. A pastor needs to fully teach the compassion of God and understand what is being taught in the corners or *'unbelieving-excuse making'* television ministries so they won't wonder why they don't get the manifestations of power that God wills. United we will stand and divided some will fall.

"No sooner do they hear the Word than Satan snatches away what has been planted in them." Mark 4:15 MB

"For I have not shunned to declare to you the whole counsel of God. Therefore take heed to yourselves and to all the flock, among which the Holy Spirit has made you overseers, to shepherd the church of God which He purchased with His own blood. For I know this, that after my departure savage wolves will come in among you, not sparing the flock. Also from among yourselves men will rise up, speaking perverse things, to draw away the disciples after them." Acts 20:27-30 NKJ

Some are hindered who don't know the will of God. The deficiency or unwillingness to do good for us is never in God. God loves us and wants us to receive abundant life more than we do. His conditions for healing and miracles was and is; our faith. When His will is made known, we can trust and react on it and treat God as an honest being. When a leper asked if it was his will to heal, Jesus let him know it is his will to make him clean and removed the stumbling block of ignorance with revealed knowledge. Jesus told the centurion of what He was willing to do. In our own lives we grow from; '*I think God can*' to '*I think He will*' or '*I wish He would*' to 'I know He will'

"And behold, a leper came and worshipped Him, saying, 'Lord, if you are willing, you can make me clean.' Then Jesus put out his hand and touched him, saying, '<u>I am willing</u>; be cleansed. And immediately his leprosy was cleansed." Matthew 8:2, 3 NKJ

"As Jesus entered the village of Capernaum, a Roman captain came up in a panic and said, "Master, my servant is sick. He can't walk. He's in terrible pain." Jesus said, "I'll come and heal him." Matthew 8:5-7 MB

Unforgiveness is another possible hindrance. Holding hatred in our heart was something mankind was not designed for. Chronic unforgiveness can also cause headache, neck and back pain. The self-righteousness of grudge holding prevents our spiritual connection with God. The same can be said about worrying, or meditation on the devil's promises for the future.

"For assuredly, I say to you, whoever says to this mountain, 'Be removed and be cast into the sea,' and does not doubt in his heart, but believes that those things he says will be done, he will have whatever he says. Therefore I say to you, whatever things you ask when you pray, believe that you receive *them,* and you will have *them.* And whenever you stand praying, if you have anything against anyone, forgive him, that your Father in heaven may also forgive you your trespasses." Mark 11:24-26 NKJ

Jesus made the example of teaching, preaching and healing in the cities that He went. People chose to accept it or reject it. Healing had to be received by faith;

"How then shall they call on him in whom they have not believed? and how shall they believe in him of whom they have not heard? and how shall they hear without a preacher?" Romans 10:14

The only times we've seen people not being healed was not because of God's will to heal all, but because of lack of faith, as seen in this example in the Lord's hometown;

"And he could there do no mighty work, save that he laid his hands upon a few sick folk, and healed them. And he marvelled because of their unbelief..." Mark 6:5, 6

It does not matter if you've never seen miracles and healing before. It does not change things if millions missed out on healing for centuries. Regardless of how many churches who teach that miracles are only for back then, God's name is I AM, not I *was*. We must keep holding on to His word until the manifestation of the promise is fulfilled. If we are being occupied with symptoms or feelings from the natural five senses, we waver by violating spiritual requirements and turn off the switch to His power. Hold on to your confession and no disease can stay in your presence.

"God keeps his word even when the whole world is lying through its teeth. Scripture says the same" Romans 3:5 MB

"Let us hold fast the profession of our faith with-out wavering; (for he is faithful that promised)" Hebrews 10:23

The confessions with our own mouth and even the acceptance of the negative confessions of others can put a slow down to healing. If we repeat statements like '*My back is killing me*', '*This disease runs in my family*' or '*I always get sick this time of year*' we may very well receive in faith the manifestation of a negative meditation. We should not lie and deny any symptoms, but acknowledge the Word's ability to help us. If we are to put on the whole armour of God and fight the good fight of faith with the use the Sword of the Spirit, we will be better off to eliminate the unproductive confession and apply the potential of God-given control that will make us better off. Doubt confession denies the ability and mercy of God. Openly confessing the word and promises of God brings angelic help and power of the Spirit.

"Death and life are in the power of the tongue: and they that love it will eat its fruit." **Proverbs 18:21 NKJ**

"We're not keeping this quiet, not on your life. Just like the psalmist who wrote, "I believed it, so I said it," we say what we believe." **2 Corinthians 4:13 MB**

"For he puts you under his angel's charge, to guard you wherever you go." **Psalm 91:11 Mof**

"Also I say to you, whoever confesses Me before men, him the Son of Man also will confess before the angels of God. But he who denies Me before men will be denied before the angels of God." **Luke 12:8, 9 NKJ**

Some stumble on personal types of dispensationalism resulting from poor self-esteem. They may think; *if a certain person gets healed, I'll believe.* In their minds they say; *if I see hundreds of people get healed first, then I know my healing is coming.* They may also give regard to the sin or condemnation in their heart. Because their hearts condemn them, their confidence in prayer is weakened. They become prayer cowards and double-mindedly deceive themselves, and lower the expectations of others looking for hope. Asking God for something becomes like rolling dice. They have an expectation of some form of damnation from sin-consciousness, instead of God consciousness. Even in our standards, a Father who would punish His children by making them suffer would be considered child-abuse. We are not worthy of suffering from God, so don't adopt that image of yourself. Although some may take persecution from men because of our witness, we should not mix persecution with sickness or disease. God doesn't change or have a performance orientated reward or punishment conditions. If you think evil is for your own good, than you won't have confidence in prayer and receiving.

"For we walk by faith, not by sight" 2 Corinthians 5:7

"Had I been thinking secretly of sin, the Lord would never have listened" Psalm 66:18 Mof

"For if our heart condemns us, God is greater than our heart, and knows all things. Beloved, if our heart does not condemn us, we have confidence toward God. And whatever we ask we receive from Him, because we keep His commandments and do those things that are pleasing in His sight." I John 3:20-22 NKJ

"For God did not send His Son into the world to condemn the world, but that the world through Him might be saved. He who believes in Him is not condemned; but he who does not believe is condemned already..." John 3:17, 18 NKJ

If King David could show great mercy towards Saul, after attempted murder and even willing to die for a son that betrayed him (1 Sam 26:11, 2 Sam 18:33, 19:5, 6) and the angel Michael, reflecting the harmony in heaven did not even accuse the devil, how much greater then, is God's love and willingness to extend mercy toward us?

"But even Michael, one of the mightiest of the angels, did not dare accuse the devil of blasphemy, but simply said, 'The Lord rebuke you!' (This took place when Michael was arguing with the devil about Moses' body.)" Jude 1:9 NLT

God doesn't create diseases or have any use for it. He only wants His children to have abundant life; unlike the *thief*. If God wants to give good things to His children and give them soon, how much longer would you think He wants to wait? We are not here to fully figure out God, but to know His characteristics, nature, and what He wants for our lives. Even as the Spirit has given us instruction to give what is due, He does not want to hold back anything from us.

"Do not withhold good from those to whom it is due, when it is in the power of your hand to do *so*. Do not say to your neighbor, 'Go, and come back, and tomorrow I will give *it,'* When *you have* it with you." Proverbs 3:27, 28 NKJ

"Leave no debt unpaid except the standing debt of mutual love." Romans 13:7, 8 Wey

There are also doctrines that men and false prophets have been preaching for a long time. Even the disciples of Jesus supposed a blind man was faced with his condition because of his sin or the sins of his parents.

"And his disciples asked him, saying, 'Rabbi, who sinned, this man or his parents, that he was born blind? Jesus answered, "Neither this man nor his parents sinned, but that the works of God should be revealed in him." John 9:2, 3 NKJ

Some people have been taught that '*God is in control of the devil or has the devil on a lease'*. The devil behind this preaching would have you think you are powerless and that God will do all the work for you. Jesus administered victorious authority rule over spirits. If God was going to do it himself, there was no need to tell us or his disciples to do it.

We are here to take control with the authority He has given us. We are the final say so to what happens to us in our life, lest Satan take <u>advantage</u> of us. The '*god*' of this world only rules in his dominion.

"And the seventy returned again with joy, saying, Lord, even the devils are subject unto us through thy name. And he said unto them, I beheld Satan as lightning fall from heaven. Behold, I give unto you power to tread on serpents and scorpions, and over all the power of the enemy: and nothing shall by any means hurt you. Notwithstanding in this rejoice not, that the spirits are subject unto you; but rather rejoice, because your names are written in heaven." Luke 10:17-20

"Lest Satan should get an advantage of us: for we are not ignorant of his devices." 2 Corinthians 2:11

In generations of ignorance, slothfulness, chosen irre-sponsibility, and dependency, many have claimed; '*God is in control of everything*' as if God contributes to the works of the devil directly or indirectly. This statement would mean he is in control over starvation, rape, poverty, pre-mature death etc. But we know there's a thief. So, give no place to the devil. <u>You</u> have to put on the armour of God. <u>You</u> have to renew your mind and walk in the spirit. <u>You</u> will speak to the mountain. What you believe or don't believe will limit God's manifestations in your life. It will either give the devil a foothold or take away the devil's hold on your life. The devil is afraid of a person with power or one who believes in God's word and uses their natural authority given to them from the Lord.

"Don't give the Devil that kind of foothold in your life." Ephesians 4:27

"The thief does not come except to steal, and to kill, and to destroy. I have come that they may have life, and that they may have *it* more abundantly." John 10:10 NKJ

Another similar false doctrine is '*nothing happens to you unless God allows it*'. This destructive *sermon* has made some mad at God, making them believe God <u>allows</u> things to happen but, all along it is an invisible devil. It would make you have questions like "*Why did <u>God</u> let my son die*?" But, God is not an ACCOMPLICE (*i.e. a person involved in a crime but did not pull the trigger*). He is not in agreement by ALLOWING the devil to do evil things. God is not in control of the decisions <u>we</u> make or the devil's decisions, or the results that come with them. The devil doesn't seek who he wants to devour, but who allows him to. Resist the devil and he will flee from you. There are times when it is not enough to resist temptation, but to tell the devil to go. Even so, there are times a devil must be ejected before a healing can take place.

"Be well balanced (temperate, sober of mind), be vigilant and cautious at all times; for that enemy of yours, the devil, roams around like a lion roaring [in fierce hunger], seeking someone to seize upon and devour" 1 Peter 5:8 AMP

"Therefore submit to God. Resist the devil and he will flee from you." James 4:7 NKJ

"There is a way *that seems* right to a man, But its end *is* the way of death." Proverbs 14:12 NKJ

Although they are fading fast, other popular phrases that have echoed in many churches and pulpits include '*God makes people sick, or he gets glory out of sickness, or he uses sickness to teach you a lesson, get your attention or keep you humble and uses it to get you closer to him'.* These events would make God actively or passively behind the scenes of sickness, leading people to believe that God makes people sick and not the devil, so you would not cast the devil out. If God wanted you to be sick, Jesus must have been working against him by healing. God is not in collaboration with the devil to make us sick or teach us lessons. If people don't fill their temple (body) with the Word of God, the devil could take advantage of them, manifesting <u>his</u> will through people. If you thought that God made people sick to make them humble; you would not stop <u>HIM</u>. However, if you knew that the devil was the cause, <u>you would</u> cast him out. Jesus spoke of demons and the authority we have here *more* than heaven or hell. The Holy Spirit can teach you more about being humble than any infirmity. God gets glory out of *overcoming* sickness and death and is responsible for backing up the Word with the anecdote through the anointing He's given us. We can use our power by rightly dividing the truth.

"Humble yourselves therefore under the mighty hand of God, that he may exalt you in due time" 1 Peter 5:6

"And have put on the new man, which is renewed in knowledge after the image of him that created him" Colossians 3:10

"However, when He, the Spirit of truth, has come, He will guide you into all truth; for He will not speak on His own *authority,* but whatever He hears He will speak; and He will tell you things to come." John 16:13 NKJ

Some have attempted to introduce the hypothetical to the Word; *'If the Lord wants to heal you He can', 'it's in the Lord's hands', 'if it's meant to happen it will'.* The 'if' indicates the possibility of Him <u>not</u> wanting to heal the people He was sent to die for. He searches for our faith. Whether a need for healings or revivals, our time of dependency on the rare sovereign moves of God will be replaced by the Godly moves on our part. Heaven is in God's hands. The earth is in turmoil and conflict. We have a covenant with God that is not one-sided and requires two parties. If you're not using your faith in connection with a promise, then the situation is up for grabs. We need to fight as soldiers for the body of Christ.

"Bless the LORD, O my soul, And forget not all His benefits: Who forgives all your iniquities, Who heals all your diseases" Psalm 103:2, 3 NKJ

"Surely he has borne our griefs and carried our sorrows; yet we esteemed him stricken, smitten of God, and afflicted. But he was wounded for our transgressions, he was bruised for our iniquities: the chastisement for our peace was upon him; and by his stripes we are healed." Isaiah 53:4, 5 NKJ

"Then touched he their eyes, saying, According to your faith be it unto you." Matthew 9:29

"Fight the good fight of faith, lay hold on eternal life, to which you were also called and have confessed the good confession in the presence of many witnesses." 1 Timothy 6:12 NKJ

There are also speculations from those who say *'everything happens in the Lord's time' or 'just wait on the Lord'*. The lazy spirit of procrastination wants to make God's chosen put off responsibility. The answer to His promises are always yes, but we've seen the manifestation of some things delayed in Old Testament times by the enemy on the outside, and after the opposition was defeated on the cross, the enemy on the inside (*the fleshly way of thinking*) that has been fed with powerless theology. People may experience delays in time according to their faith in what they've been hearing. A lot of delayed theology needs to be uprooted. Even when we wait on the Lord, as described in the 40th chapter of Isaiah, the kind of waiting according to the literal Hebrew text does not imply a passive experience, but being active in the same way a 'waiter' would on his job. When Jesus said 'it is finished' it was really finished. There is much more work we need to do on our part through faith and utterance.

"For all of God's promises have been fulfilled in Christ with a resounding Yes!" 2 Corinthians 1:20 NLT

"Then he said to me, "Do not fear, Daniel, for from the first day that you set your heart to understand, and to humble yourself before your God, your words were heard; and I have come because of your words. But the prince of the kingdom of Persia withstood me twenty-one days; and behold, Michael, one of the chief princes, came to help me, for I had been left alone there with the kings of Persia." Daniel 10:12, 13 NKJ

"Having disarmed principalities and powers, He made a public spectacle of them, triumphing over them in it." Colossians 2:15 NKJ

"So when Jesus had received the sour wine, He said, "It is finished!" And bowing His head, He gave up His Spirit." John 19:30 NKJ

"But those who wait upon the Lord- [who expect, look for, and hope in Him] shall change and renew their strength and power.; they shall lift their wings and mount up

[close to God] as eagles [mount up to the sun] they shall run and not be weary, they shall walk and not faint or become tired." Isaiah 40:31 AMP

A familiar stumbling block is the old saying *'the Lord has not promised us tomorrow.' Or 'it might be your time to go'.* This is a bad thing to believe that when you're sick. There is only hopelessness in this phrase. A lifetime of believing and speaking this with the addition to giving up an 'Amen' to other people that proclaim this is more anthropological than spiritual. It's more humanistic than supernatural. If all heaven and hell are fighting for us, we should not give any opportunities in our speech to make our life up for grabs. When we become supernatural spiritual beings, then we should walk by faith and not by sight. Even if many Christian soldiers have circumstances that went on for millenniums, we can choose to believe the experience of life or the infallibility of the Word. We can recognize and accept our spiritual promises, or leave this planet the same way some of our ancestors did.

"And the LORD said, My spirit shall not always strive with man, for that he also is flesh: yet his days shall be an hundred and twenty years." Genesis 6:3

"Do not be overly wicked, Nor be foolish: Why should you die before your time?" Ecclesiastes 7:17 NKJ

"With long life will I satisfy him, and show him my salvation." Psalm 91:16 NKJ

"And we have received God's Spirit (not the world's spirit), so we can know the wonderful things God has freely given us. When we tell you these things, we do not use words that come from human wisdom. Instead, we speak words given to us by the Spirit, using the Spirit's words to

explain spiritual truths. But people who aren't spiritual can't receive these truths from God's Spirit. It all sounds foolish to them and they can't understand it, for only those who are spiritual can understand what the Spirit means." 1 Corinthians 2:12-14 NKJ

In mono-verso theology, certain men have made the body of Christ stall for time in taking verses out of context to explain their own reason for suffering. In other words, people use one verse of the bible to justify their way of thinking because it is easier for some to believe if it happened to a biblical person, it could happen to me. A popular verse that ignores the rest of the book that Job is proclaiming out of ignorance is '*the good Lord giveth and the good Lord taketh away*'. Job could not read the first two chapters of his own book like we can and realize Satan was the cause of his problems. We can see an open invitation to the enemy by Job to give up his hedge from having the spirit of fear and the Lord observing this knew that he was in the hands of Satan.

"For the thing which I greatly feared is come upon me, and that which I was afraid of is come unto me. I was not in safety, neither had I rest, neither was I quiet; yet trouble came." Job 3:25, 26

"...he also himself likewise took part of the same; that through death he might destroy him that had the power of death, that is, the devil; And deliver them who through fear of death were all their lifetime subject to bondage." Hebrews 2:14, 15

"For God hath not given us the spirit of fear; but of power, and of love, and of a sound mind." 2 Timothy 1:7

Job complained and blamed God for circumstances and even said God laughs at our trials;

"For He crushes me with a tempest, And multiplies my wounds without cause. He will not allow me to catch my breath, But fills me with bitterness…" Job 9:17, 18 NKJ

"I am blameless, yet I do not know myself; I despise my life. It is all one thing; Therefore I say, 'He destroys the blameless and the wicked.' If the scourge slays suddenly, He laughs at the plight of the innocent." Job 9:21-23 NKJ

Elihu corrected him by the Spirit and God confirmed his lack of knowledge before Job finally admitted his inappropriate words. You can choose to learn from ignorant Job, or repentant Job;

"Therefore Job opens his mouth in vain; He multiplies words without knowledge." Job 35:16

"Who *is* this who darkens counsel by words without knowledge?" Job 38:2

"*You asked*, 'Who is he that hides counsel without knowledge?' Therefore have I uttered what I did not understand, things too wonderful for me, which I did not know." Job 42:3

Another singled out verse is Paul's thorn in the flesh in 2 Cor 12:7. In the original Greek where we see the word 'it' in most versions, is actually in the masculine tense as seen in the Kenneth Weust expanded version. We know *who* his thorn was (*not what*), because he describes what the messenger of Satan was doing to him. When he prayed about the messenger of Satan to stop maltreating or buffeting

(Greek-kolaphizo; to rap with the fist) him, it was like saying *'Lord let the devil stop beating me'*. We've seen Paul get beaten by many who tried to stop his message from God from being heard. The devil wanted to persecute Paul because his words of life offered help to those opposed to the devil and would have exalted his position above measure. If anyone knew who Paul's thorn was, he did himself. He described what was happening in the previous chapter. Some people who are not a threat to the devil's plans claim they have a thorn and have never even led a person to the Lord or given out a tract of the gospel.

"And respect to the super abundance of the revelations, in order that I may not be exalted overmuch, there was given to me a thorn in the flesh, a messenger of Satan, to the end that he might constantly maltreat me lest I be exalted overmuch. Concerning this three times I begged the Lord that <u>he</u> might depart from me." 2 Corinthians 12:7, 8 KW

"Are they ministers of Christ?—I speak as a fool—I *am* more: in labors more abundant, in stripes above measure, in prisons more frequently, in deaths often. From the Jews five times I received forty *stripes* minus one. Three times I was beaten with rods; once I was stoned; three times I was shipwrecked; a night and a day I have been in the deep; *in* journeys often, *in* perils of waters, *in* perils of robbers, *in* perils of *my own* countrymen, *in* perils of the Gentiles, *in* perils in the city, *in* perils in the wilderness, *in* perils in the sea, *in* perils among false brethren..." 2 Corinthians 11:23-26 NKJ

If people think that God is the one who allows the devil to have freewill on our lives or there's a possibility that He won't heal us, this will be a stumbling block that's hard to penetrate. We have to learn the enemies' *wiles* or *methods* causing folks to fall. They may say a particular disease is *'their cross to bear'*. The trials are not our cross, so people should not carry Satan's burdens. The <u>cross</u> is the message of the good news that says 'I (*the old man*) am crucified with Christ and carry this cross daily'. So every time the old man in you says; I'm sick, or I'm weak; you can say to the old man 'you've died and now Christ lives in me' and claim your blessings from our Father.

"Put on all of God's armor so that you will be able to stand firm against all strategies of the devil. For we are not fighting against flesh-and-blood enemies, but against evil rulers and authorities of the unseen world, against mighty powers in this dark world, and against evil spirits in the heavenly places." Ephesians 6:11, 12 NLT

Some people become suffering minded because they take the scripture in Hebrews out of context;

"Though he were a Son, yet learned he obedience by the things which he suffered" Hebrews 5:8

This would mean that he would have been disobedient at sometime, contrary to the word. This could mean you would learn by suffering instead of God's Holy Spirit. God does not use suffering to teach you. Jesus was obedient from infancy to the cross. Since He was God and did not know *experientially* what it was like being a human, led by the Spirit, battling spiritual battles, obeying the Father with faith trust; in order for Jesus to become high priest forever. We would not have a high priest if He didn't. Trials don't come from God, but His children have Authority over the trial givers. He experienced obedience from man's point of view. The trials are not more precious than gold, our <u>faith</u> is. Jesus was and is perfect.

"That the trial of your faith, being much more precious than of gold..." 1 Peter 1:7

How many times have you heard some people say '*We all have our weaknesses*'? This could be '*a truth*' but may not be the whole truth. Be strong in the power of His might. You won't possess weakness if you walk in the spirit. You may encounter them, but they are not legally yours. Some could be weak from taking communion unworthily. There are also those who take heed to unbelievers, who are not strong in the miracle power of God. Others may feel weak and allow their emotions to rule instead of God. Let the weak say I'm strong!

"For if you eat the bread or drink the cup without honoring the body of Christ, you are eating and drinking God's judgment upon yourself. That is why many of you are weak and sick and some have even died." 1 Corinthians 11:29, 30 NKJ

"Don't become partners with those who reject God. How can you make a partnership out of right and wrong? That's not partnership; that's war" 2 Corinthians 6:14 MB

"I say then: Walk in the Spirit, and you shall not fulfill the lust of the flesh." Galatians 5:16 NKJ

"Finally, my brethren, be strong in the Lord, and in the power of his might." Ephesians 6:10

There are some who don't receive the *true* messenger or know the reward that comes with it. You should have a peace in your heart for legitimate fruit or heed internal spiritual warning signs for ungodly people. A person may appear strange and certainly we are all not infallible, but we can look for an anointing in people without judging them to pull out of them what God has chosen them for. We can miss out on much, if we reject different parts of the body. The Corinthian church were full of gifts, but took time to develop maturity. There are even those who have slipped away but have repented. We know God does not take back gifts, but will wash us all with the water of the Word. Edification can be obtained by recognizing the anointing instead of the outward appearance.

"If you receive a prophet as one who speaks for God, you will be given the same reward as a prophet. And if you receive righteous people because of their righteousness, you will be given a reward like theirs." Matthew 10:41 NKJ

"...Hear me, O Judah, and ye inhabitants of Jerusalem; Believe in the LORD your God, so shall ye be established; believe his prophets, so shall ye prosper." 2 Chronicles 20:20

"Beloved, believe not every spirit, but try the spirits whether they are of God: because many false prophets are gone out into the world." 1 John 4:1

"For as the body is one, and hath many members, and all the members of that one body, being many, are one body: so also is Christ....that there should be no schism in the body; but that the members should have the same care one for another. And whether one member suffer, all the

members suffer with it; or one member be honoured, all the members rejoice with it. Now ye are the body of Christ, and members in particular." 1 Corinthians 12:12, 25-27

"...The things which God cleansed, as for you, stop declaring unhallowed" Acts 10:15 (KW)

"When they arrived, Samuel took one look at Eliab and thought, 'Surely this is the Lord's anointed!' But the Lord said to Samuel, 'Don't judge by his appearance or height, for I have rejected him. The Lord doesn't see things the way you see them. People judge by outward appearance, but the Lord looks at the heart.' " 1 Samuel 16:6, 7 NKJ

Some people may shortcut the healing process by stopping medication for ailments. Unless God personally gives us a specific current word on a situation, we should be comforted with His way to heal us. We may not know how He will, but we know that He will. Our minds should be exercised into following God and be open to His ways of healing. If we don't get immediate results, medication should be continued until the condition is totally gone. God may tell us to use medicine, or the things that are already around us. Even our own bodies have the healing design of God within themselves; like when our skin gets cut. It is good to see a doctor for confirmation and testimony that the matter is disappeared or reduced over time. We've seen men of God use earthly medicinal remedies of nature to help ailments in the bible and in Luke's account, the Lord sent the leper to the priests for a testimony;

"And his servants came near and spoke to him, and said, "My father, *if* the prophet had told you *to do* something great, would you not have done *it*? How much more then, when he says to you, 'Wash, and be clean'?"

So he went down and dipped seven times in the Jordan, according to the saying of the man of God; and his flesh was restored like the flesh of a little child, and he was clean." 2 Kings 5:13, 14 NKJ

"Return and tell Hezekiah the leader of My people, 'Thus says the LORD, the God of David your father: 'I have heard your prayer, I have seen your tears; surely I will heal you. On the third day you shall go up to the house of the LORD. And I will add to your days fifteen years... Then Isaiah said, "Take a lump of figs." So they took and laid *it* on the boil, and he recovered." 2 Kings 20:5-7 NKJ

"Go ahead and drink a little wine, for instance; it's good for your digestion, good medicine for what ails you." 1 Timothy 5:23 MB

"Then He put out *His* hand and touched him, saying, "I am willing; be cleansed." Immediately the leprosy left him. And He charged him to tell no one, "But go and show yourself to the priest, and make an offering for your cleansing, as a testimony to them, just as Moses commanded." Luke 5:13, 14 NKJ

We have the Spirit of God to personally lead us in the right things to do when we listen. There are many circumstances that require our obedience first. A relationship with God takes time to know His heart and depend on His personal instructions. Some time ago, there was a time when I had been shaking hands with someone who has a common cold. The Lord simply told me to wash my hands. In my mind I said 'I'll just rebuke any symptoms that come as usual and *then* nip it in the bud. I had to battle with sniffles later on that night. Another time I was having a headache. I rebuked and it left. It came back. I rebuked it again until it left. It came back a third time. Before I could even get the prayer out, the Lord spoke to me and said; "Your glasses are too tight!" As the old saying goes; *'an ounce of prevention is worth a pound of cure'*. When something is not handled right away, your flesh, feelings and emotions will draw on unbelief and it will be more challenging to your faith and in time, may develop a spiritual callous in your mind that needs to be destroyed. Our mind needs to feed on His words for direction for the most efficient way of receiving from Him.

"Trust God from the bottom of your heart; don't try to figure out everything on your own. Listen for God's voice in everything you do, everywhere you go; he's the one who will keep you on track. Don't assume that you know it all. Run to God! Run from evil! Your body will glow with health; your very bones will vibrate with life!" Proverbs 3:5-8 MB

For centuries after the great works of the apostles, there was good ground to sow the healing seeds of the Word to us, but weeds were formed by the limited access to the Word for laymen, or preachers who perverted the gospel. Paul repeated messages about people who did these things even when he was around. Angels were also potential messengers of Satan. Islam and Mormonism began when men heard angels speak to them. Their doctrines became far from God's teaching on healing. Today, more people have access to good bibles, receive much more preaching on healing and we hear and witness a greater amount of healings and miracles than there has ever been. Even those who haven't reached the creative miracles have at least enough faith for healing and are on their way to greater works. If things don't happen right away, never let the failure stop you. Use it as a stepping stone to wait on God's direction with patience. Disease is a physical manifestation of collective beliefs over millenniums. We need to hear more Word on and have more guidance to tip the scale in our understanding. When we think more about what He is more than willing to do in our lives we will be better at receiving. The power of the blood of Jesus is so much greater than anything that Adam had sold us out to.

"But while men slept, his enemy came and sowed tares among the wheat, and went his way. But when the blade was sprung up, and brought forth fruit, then appeared the tares also." Matthew13:26, 27

"Study and be eager and do your utmost to present yourself to God approved (tested by trial), a work-man who has no cause to be ashamed, correctly analyzing and accurately dividing [rightly hand-ling and skillfully teaching] the Word of Truth." 2 Timothy 2:15 AMP

"...there be some that trouble you, and would per-vert the gospel of Christ. But though we, or an angel from heaven, preach any other gospel unto you than that which we have preached unto you, let him be accursed. As we said before, so say I now again, If any man preach any other gospel unto you than that ye have received, let him be accursed. For do I now persuade men, or God? or do I seek to please men?" Galatians 1:7-10

"who Himself bore our sins in His own body on the tree, that we, having died to sins, might live for righteousness — by whose stripes you were healed." 1 Peter 2:24 NKJ

Today, some people within the church are still sowing bad seeds for personal gain, attention or addiction to self-righteousness. There are many who have had physically or mentally abusive fathers who were selfish, unaffectionate, and were controlled by the lust of the eyes and flesh. When these see the word father in the bible, they have a hard time relating to a God that loves and desires to make one whole. Many of them become suffering minded and teach others of the same expectancy.

"And, ye fathers, provoke not your children to wrath: but bring them up in the nurture and admonition of the Lord." Ephesians 6:4

"*There is* a generation *that* curses its father, And does not bless its mother. *There is* a generation *that is* pure in its own eyes, *Yet* is not washed from its filthiness." Proverbs 30:11, 12 NKJ

"Furthermore we have had fathers of our flesh which corrected us, and we gave them reverence: shall we not much rather be in subjection unto the Father of spirits, and live? For they verily for a few days chastened us after their own pleasure; but he for our profit, that we might be partakers of his holiness." Hebrews 12:9, 10

One worse case spiritual scenario is to see doctor's but avoid God's word altogether;

"In the thirty-ninth year of his reign, Asa developed a serious foot disease. Yet even with the severity of his disease, he did not seek the Lord's help but turned only to his physicians. So he died in the forty-first year of his reign." 2 Chronicles 16:12, 13 NLT

If you are ruled by walking by sight, it's unscientific because it does not take into account all the facts. It overlooks the Champion of all facts. God would be unjust to withhold promises from us, but He is faithful and just. Again, a symptom may be '*a truth*', but shouldn't make you deny 'the Truth' that you are healed and all the enemy has to threaten you with is temporary. God has given us over to life instead of the deadly rule of the world. He has given us authorization to do things quickly. To cash in on our redemption, we must take the Word of God at face value and shorten the time of manifestation as much as possible.

"Jesus said to him, "I am the way, the truth, and the life. No one comes to the Father except through Me." John 14:6 NKJ

"For You, Lord, *are* good, and ready to forgive, And abundant in mercy to all those who call upon You." Psalm 86:5 NKJ

We can cash in on our redemption anytime because of what the Lord has already done. Satan's dominion is over! When we get in our minds the ease of healing and the church as a whole gets used to the planting of this good seed, God will give the increase to this faith and we will walk easier in the path of creative and instantaneous miracles. We can depend on God to use His 'miracle grow' power as the greatest Farmer in the universe!

"I have planted, Apollos watered; but God gave the increase." 1 Corinthians 3:6

"Therefore be patient, brethren, until the coming of the Lord. See *how* the farmer waits for the precious fruit of the earth, waiting patiently for it until it receives the early and latter rain." James 5:7 NKJ

CHAPTER 6

Instruments of War

"But when a stronger than he comes upon him and over-comes him, he takes from him all his armor in which he trusted, and divides his spoils. He who is not with Me is against Me, and he who does not gather with Me scatters." Luke 11:22-23 NKJ

Adam was born immortal. He had never suffered sickness, disease, weather conditions or anything under the curse of the law. When he fell to an announcement of the enemy, he was spoiled of his instruments of spiritual warfare into a corrupted environment.

"The tools of our trade aren't for marketing or manipulation, but they are for demolishing that entire massively corrupt culture." 2 Corinthians 10:4 MB

He placed a value on a second opinion and was talked out of his authority;

"Wherefore, as by one man sin entered into the world, and death by sin; and so death passed upon all men, for that all have sinned" Romans 5:12

He never knew condemnation, but got more than a simple speech from the enemy after making a crucial mistake that would affect the whole world. The earth would have to wait to be replenished (Gen 1:28).

The enemy had a history of giving men words to have individualism by his divisional tactics;

"The LORD said to him, 'In what way?' So he said, 'I will go out and be a lying spirit in the mouth of all his prophets.' And the LORD said, 'You shall persuade *him, and also prevail. Go out and do so." 1 Kings 22:22 KJV

From the time of Cain to the time of Moses, few people showed evidence of receiving God's word and lived it. Few people shook off the thoughts of the enemy and verbal condemnation and showed the boldness of unseen God given power. Most others who were around the opportunity to have spiritual increase with the Word in synagogues and churches have had bad teaching and mediocrity at best, not honoring the instruction and correction of God's prophets. Many churches today still have the same 6,000 year old expectancies of defeat, suffering and condemnation the world system offers without remedy from God. Men like Elijah and Elisha knew about the availability of this authority that was a provision for men, before the appearance of Jesus. He tells men of this authority in the prophecy of Jeremiah;

"You *are* My battle-ax *and* weapons of war: For with you I will break the nation in pieces; With you I will destroy kingdoms" Jeremiah 51:20 NKJ

Jesus came to give an example of showing this authority given to men. The enemy never had the right to have it. He doesn't have the right to keep it. Jesus was not always as peaceful as an artist would paint Him to be. There are times He comes as a champion, leading us for battle, who always has an army of angels ready to fight. These are not like the wimpy baby angels you may have seen drawings of, but angels strong enough to roll a big stone away (John 20:1) or wipe out thousands (Isaiah 37:36) at one time;

"Now I saw heaven opened, and behold, a white horse. And He who sat on him *was* called Faithful and True, and in righteousness He judges and makes war...and His name is called The Word of God. And the armies in heaven, clothed in fine linen, white and clean, followed Him on white horses. Now out of His mouth goes a sharp sword, that with it He should strike the nations. And He Himself will rule them with a rod of iron..." Revelation 19:11-15 NKJ

"Don't you realize that I am able right now to call to my Father, and twelve companies—more, if I want them—of fighting angels would be here, battle-ready?" Matthew 26:53 MB

We spoil the enemy by taking back the authority Jesus said we have;

"And these signs shall follow them that believe; In my name shall they cast out devils; they shall speak with new tongues; They shall take up serpents; and if they drink any deadly thing, it shall not hurt them; they shall lay hands on the sick, and they shall recover." Mark 16:17, 18

The disciples did it around Him on His word that it was possible;

"...they joyfully reported to him, "Lord, even the demons obey us when we use your name!" "Yes," he told them, "I saw Satan fall from heaven like lightning! Look, I have given you authority over all the power of the enemy, and you can walk among snakes and scorpions and crush them. Nothing will injure you." Luke 10:17-19 NLT

He gave his Holy Spirit to the apostles who demonstrated the power that God had given to men;

"Also a multitude gathered from the surrounding cities to Jerusalem, bringing sick people and those who were tormented by unclean spirits, and they were all healed." Acts 5:16 NKJ

When you receive the revelation of how defeated the enemy really is, you will use what you have been freely given. Today, with the leading of the Spirit and the Presence of God in **your** words, you can take back these instruments of war from an enemy that was defeated long ago on the cross;

"Think of it! All sins forgiven, the slate wiped clean, that old arrest warrant canceled and nailed to Christ's cross. He stripped all the spiritual tyrants in the universe of their sham authority at the Cross and marched them naked through the streets." Colossians 2:15 MB

Our belief system starts with the mind's perception of the Lord and treating Him like an honest being. He has given us the Word to show us who we really are. There are forces that whisper to you and try to lead you into their pathways like *anger, guilt, covetousness, greed, gluttony, pride, lust, laziness* or *anything* that your adversary will attempt to make you identify with or justify the identity they want to give you. Just like God has a 'rhema' or living word, the enemy will have an *active temptation* to entice you to sin. After one accepts this deception, he will try to include seven other spirits of *shame, doubt, lying, unbelieving, procrastinating, rebellion* and *condemning spirits*. The devil cannot repent because he didn't have a tempter like we have, but we can stop allowing any form of condemnation from the adversary to 'hold water'. Through the blood of Jesus, his children are guilt free in the eyes of God and can always repent, or change their behavior. We can rest in the identity of who God says we are and what He says we can do. He plants seeds within you to grow into who He has called you to be. You will see things as God does. You will see into the invisible beyond the unchangeable. The more you hear His Word, the more you will stay anchored in what He believes in.

"But each one is tempted when he is drawn away by his own desires and enticed. Then, when desire has conceived, it gives birth to sin; and sin, when it is full-grown, brings forth death." James 1:14, 15 NKJ

"Then he goes and takes with him seven other spirits more wicked than himself, and they enter and dwell there; and the last *state* of that man is worse than the first. So shall it also be with this wicked generation." Matthew 12:45 NKJ

"Set your affection on things above, not on things on the earth." Colossians 3:2

We are all called to meet our enemy face to face and use our light to defeat darkness. Spiritual warfare is not for us to get the victory, but to keep it. Demonic forces will test you and do spiritual background checks on you. They'll see if you're serious. They may check your history and see if the spirit of doubt, fear or worry were able to distract you so they could use them again. They'll check the words of your mouth because you'll testify what you've been thinking and what you believe in. They'll try to put words in your mouth knowing someone is looking up to you for inspiration. The enemy wants to give you his vision and try to make you think you don't have victory, but you are not here to tolerate his behavior in your atmosphere or circle of great spiritual influence. You are not here to accept his *depreciation*, but God's appreciation of you. Whenever you feel anyone or anything telling you something different than what God's love, Spirit and Word tells you, just stand on God's Word. Great faith is not so much as a great moment of faith, but keeping a continuous victorious belief until your last enemy has fallen.

"But though we, or an angel from heaven, preach any other gospel unto you than that which we have preached unto you, let him be accursed. As we said before, so say I now again, If any man preach any other gospel unto you than that ye have received, let him be accursed." Galatians 1:8, 9

"But thanks *be* to God, who gives us the victory through our Lord Jesus Christ. Therefore, my beloved brethren, be steadfast, immovable, always abounding in the work of the Lord, knowing that your labor is not in vain in the Lord." 1 Corinthians 15:57, 58 NKJ

Disease is a physical manifestation of collective beliefs. If you think your experience and what you've heard happen to people over the last six millenniums is greater than the

106

teaching of the Holy Spirit, you will immediately fall short of the glory of God. If you think age, circumstances, or the roll of the dice events are to be put up with, you may *'give it a pass'* in your life especially if you see other peers or things that *'ran in the family'* and accepted the same manifestations from the world system of beliefs. The world system from the *'god of this world'* represents a complete illusion of make believe or *'make you believe'* circumstances from his teaching that came from the beginning. He wants to devour anyone who will allow him to. He wants to steer anyone away from the Anecdote and make them feel guilty, unworthy and procrastinate talking with God and reading the bible. The plan was to make men fail, keep them failing and have men to teach others to accept the attitude of failure. The devil's plan for the church was for men to tolerate at least a few things, compromise or just get by. This is not the plan of God. All manifested plans that are alien to God are illegitimate experiences. If you think these things are your lot in life, you will confess it and have bodily destruction. If you let God rule your thoughts and confession, you will live under the law of the Spirit of Life.

"The Devil is poised to pounce, and would like nothing better than to catch you napping. Keep your guard up. You're not the only ones plunged into these hard times. It's the same with Christians all over the world" 1 Peter 5:8, 9 MB

"By our speech we can ruin the world, turn harmony to chaos, throw mud on a reputation, send the whole world up in smoke and go up in smoke with it, smoke right from the pit of hell." James 3:6 MB

"A new power is in operation. The Spirit of life in Christ, like a strong wind, has magnificently cleared the air,

freeing you from a fated lifetime of brutal tyranny at the hands of sin and death." Romans 8:2 MB

If a feeling of sickness, nausea or pain comes suddenly upon you, you need to rebuke it before your senses; feelings, emotions or feelings in your body and mind try to get you to accept it. Your body and mind trust walking not only by sight (*and not faith*) but smell, taste, touch and feeling. Develop a practice of walking by your sixth sense of Faith. This will eventually rule over your whole being. When you can nip it the bud with God's word and promise, you won't have to fight with your ever-present flesh that has more time to deceive you more than the devil does. In practice, you'll learn to ward off anything from sniffles to stubbed toes while increasing your faith to uproot what your mind may have accepted for years but deep inside, your spirit man knew better. You can exercise your senses to operate faster than scientists can make up a name for a '*new*' disease. Even if you're a woman, you can realize God's desire was not for you to suffer in labor, or other things. The removal of the curse was not only for Adam. The blood of Jesus is more powerful than anything those two ever did! Your 'work' is to believe. In my family, there was a generational curse that took away an older sister at birth, had my brother and I born premature and threatened to take away the life from my niece's baby according to the doctor's report. After the prayer of faith was prayed, she had a full term healthy baby and the labor was only a few minutes! When you stack up deposits of faith from the Word in your spiritual bank account and keep your deposits in there with accepting meditation, you will 'earn' manifestations in your life with a God who has great 'interest' in you. Let His word in you be more powerful than your feelings.

"So I say, let the Holy Spirit guide your lives..." Galatians 5:16 NLT

"But be doers of the word, and not hearers only, deceiving yourselves." James 1:22 NKJ

"Jesus answered and said to them, "This is the work of God, that you believe in Him whom He sent." John 6:29 NKJ

"But we're not quitters who lose out. Oh, no! We'll stay with it and survive, trusting all the way." Hebrews 10:38 MB

We are God indwelled champions with power. A champion is one who doesn't magnify the rapture above Calvary to change us; but knows the blood is power for the now. A champion in the faith is one who bears God's voice. A champion is a believer. A champion is aware of the indwelling at all times, knowing that there are ever-present spiritual weapons of mass destruction at their disposal. A champion anchors their soul unto the Lord and claims victory even when it looks like they're down. A champion knows that all darkness comes to an end and even like a seed that can grow after being dormant for thousands of years, there is nothing that can stop the life of God in them. They have the 'Now' armour of God for today's needs. A God filled champion is not intimidated by death, disease or tumors the size of watermelons. A blood bought champion not only has proved the defeat of his enemy, but has also conquered him. Champions wake up in the morning and demons tremble. Champions know that His righteousness is their righteousness. His health is their health. His peace is their peace.

"...weeping may endure for a night, but joy comes in the morning." Psalm 30:5 NKJ

"So, what do you think? With God on our side like this, how can we lose? If God didn't hesitate to put everything on the line for us, embracing our condition and exposing himself to the worst by sending his own Son, is there anything else he wouldn't gladly and freely do for us? And who would dare tangle with God by messing with one of God's chosen? Who would dare even to point a finger?" Romans 8:31, 32 MB

Because death and life are in the power of the tongue (Prov. 18:21), God wanted us to have the creative life in our words ever since the days when Adam named the animals. When Moses came on the scene, all God had to use was a rod (Ex 4:7). From the beginning he would give excuses, ashamed of talking to Pharaoh (Ex 4:10). He didn't know the potential of his unlimited backup. He allowed God to use his rod, but held back his mouth. Whether it was used to get water from a rock, or lifted up in war, the wood 'cried out' for him (Ex 17:6, 9-11). In the day at Kadesh, God would challenge him once more to use his mouth (Ex 20:8). But, he did things the old-fashioned way and beat on it. A demonstration that would have been powerful and contagious resulted without an example of the potential power of words. These people and many others could have repeatedly and exponentially seen greater works in the lives of God's men.

Jesus taught us how to fight with words. This also works because **the enemy knows we have authority over them** and we are authorized to get things done quickly. If we confess what the world gives us, we will reap the benefits of its condemnation. When we speak confidently with our known authority, we will be justified by the righteousness of God.

"And I will give you the keys of the kingdom of heaven, and whatever you bind on earth will be bound in heaven, and whatever you loose on earth will be loosed in heaven." Matthew 16:19 NKJ

"For by your words you will be justified, and by your words you will be condemned." Matthew 12:37 NKJ

The apostles followed up with more examples for all of us who believe:

"Wherever they were scattered, they preached the Message about Jesus. Going down to a Samaritan city, Philip proclaimed the Message of the Messiah. When the people heard what he had to say and saw the miracles, the clear signs of God's action, they hung on his every word. Many who could neither stand nor walk were healed that day. The evil spirits protested loudly as they were sent on their way. And what joy in the city!" Acts 8:6-8 MB

Many men of God are following in the same footsteps today;

"Is anyone among you sick? Let him call for the elders of the church, and let them pray over him, anointing him with oil in the name of the Lord. And the prayer of faith will save the sick, and the Lord will raise him up...and pray for one another, that you may be healed. The effective, fervent prayer of a righteous man avails much." James 5:14, 15 NKJ

God gives us His Spirit to place expectancy in us. We are here to gather the spoils of the enemy like Jesus did. If we gather with him in agreement, we encourage others to come and gather. If we sit idle, the announcements that have been in books and newspapers of a *dead god*, or '*the god who used to do it*' may be the only evidence that some people will get. Don't wait for other people to step up and leave you with your talent buried. Exercise your faith and build enough spiritual muscles to extinguish any reports of the enemy.

"Who has believed our message? To whom has the Lord revealed his powerful arm?" Isaiah 53:1 NLT

Now that we've looked into the Word, and the defeat is being announced like the lepers discovering the spoils in Samaria resulting in overnight prosperity (2 Kings 7:8), we will testify what God has done with us and for us, and announce His living goodness for everyone else to gather the spoils, even if the '*chosen frozen*' speak differently (2 Kings 7:16-18). We will guard our thoughts and our heart to fight spiritually for what we believe.

"Keep your heart with all diligence, For out of it spring the issues of life." Proverbs 4:23 NKJ

"Run hard and fast in the faith. Seize the eternal life, the life you were called to, the life you so fervently embraced in the presence of so many witnesses." 1 Timothy 6:12 MB

When you walk in agreement with the Word and follow the Spirit, you will place a demand on the 'Son' kinds of results. God is already in you. We don't have to build Him or carry Him around in a temple, but we are His temple. We are not in this covenant by ourselves, but contain His more than willing power. Cancer will have to leave when you speak. Angels will have to back up God's word in you with performance. When you tell a demon to leave the angels may say to him; '*You better do what he says!*'. The tumor will become a rumor, a fever will become a 'leaver', disease will leave with ease and sickness will leave with quickness. You will use your voice mightily until you realize everything ungodly that comes into your atmosphere of experience is for you to heal, conquer and restore.

"And that about wraps it up. God is strong, and he wants you strong. So take everything the Master has set out for you, well-made weapons of the best materials. And put them to use so you will be able to stand up to everything the Devil throws your way. This is no afternoon athletic contest that we'll walk away from and forget about in a couple of hours. This is for keeps, a life-or-death fight to the finish against the Devil and all his angels." Ephesians 6:10-13 MB

CHAPTER 7

Dominion Over Time

Eternity is the face of God. Time is the face of the world. Those of us who are born again into eternity are not of the world, but are here to overcome it. Eternity does not embrace time, but we have embraced eternity. God has known you before you were an embryo and strategically placed you in this time. Before you had an opinion, God knew the choice you would make to receive Him and granted you provision through predestination. When you believe you have a role to play in the times of refreshing, you will accelerate into the supernatural and be a guide to bring others with you.

"For whatever is born of God overcomes the world. And this is the victory that has overcome the world—our faith." 1 John 5:4 NKJ

"Before I formed you in the womb I knew you; Before you were born I sanctified you; I ordained you..." Jeremiah 1:5 NKJ

"In whom also we have obtained an inheritance, being predestinated according to the purpose of him who

**worketh all things after the counsel of his own will"
Ephesians 1:11**

"... I have chosen you out of the world..." John 15:19

In the dateless past when Day and night had nothing do to with the sun, but represented events to correct the darkness on the face of the deep, God made an illuminating event of power from the beginnings of the world. This sacrifice was made in the beginning in a spiritual place called Sodom and Egypt, to replace *rebellion* and *captivity* with reunion and freedom. This was the first day that the Lord had made.

"And God called the light Day, and the darkness he called Night. And the evening and the morning were the first day." Genesis 1:5

"He who sins is of the devil, for the devil has sinned from the beginning. For this purpose the Son of God was manifested, that He might destroy the works of the devil." 1 John 3:8 NKJ

"And all that dwell upon the earth shall worship him, whose names are not written in the book of life of the Lamb slain from the foundation of the world." Revelation 13:8

"And their dead bodies shall lie in the street of the great city, which spiritually is called Sodom and Egypt, where also our Lord was crucified." Revelation 11:8

In the realm of time, the Son is known as the Alpha and Omega on the right hand of the throne. In the realm of eternity, the Father is Alpha and Omega. The Son is God's appearance in time. He is the image of the Father. He has translated us into His everlasting kingdom. He took his own royal blood into the eternal throne to release His Spirit to us. His existence has always been with us.

"I am the Alpha and the Omega...He laid His right hand on me, saying to me, "Do not be afraid; I am the First and the Last. I *am* He who lives, and was dead, and behold, I am alive forevermore..." Revelation 1:11, 17, 18 NKJ

"...in the midst of the elders, stood a Lamb as it had been slain...And he came and took the book out of the right hand of him that sat upon the throne." Revelation 5:6, 7

"The LORD said to my Lord, 'Sit at My right hand, till I make Your enemies Your footstool.'" Psalm 110:1 NKJ

"Then He who sat on the throne said, 'Behold, I make all things new'...And He said to me, 'It is done! I am the Alpha and the Omega, the Beginning and the End. I will give of the fountain of the water of life freely to him who thirsts. He who overcomes shall inherit all things, and I will be his God and he shall be My son." Revelation 21:5-7 NKJ

"In the beginning was the Word, and the Word was with God, and the Word was God... And the Word was made flesh, and dwelt among us..." John 1:1, 14

"He has delivered us from the power of darkness and conveyed *us* into the kingdom of the Son of His love, in whom we have redemption through His blood, the forgiveness of sins. He is the image of the invisible God, the firstborn over all creation. For by Him all things were created that are in heaven and that are on earth, visible and invisible, whether thrones or dominions or principalities or powers. All things were created through Him and for Him." Colossians 1:13-16 NKJ

"Jesus said to him, 'Have I been with you so long, and yet you have not known Me, Philip? He who has seen Me has seen the Father; so how can you say, 'Show us the Father?'" John 14:9 NKJ

"Jesus said to them, "Most assuredly, I say to you, before Abraham was, I AM." John 8:58 NKJ

"For thus says the LORD, Who created the heavens, Who is God, Who formed the earth and made it, Who has established it, Who did not create it in vain, Who formed it to be inhabited: 'I *am* the LORD, and *there is* no other." Isaiah 45:18 NKJ

"Neither by the blood of goats and calves, but by his own blood he entered in once into the holy place, hav-ing obtained eternal redemption for us." Hebrews 9:12

"And without controversy great is the mystery of godli-ness: God was manifest in the flesh, justified in the Spirit, seen of angels, preached unto the Gentiles, believed on in the world, received up into glory." 1 Timothy 3:16

Eternal life of the Father was manifested in you to give an inheritance of life giving dominion. You are to have rule over time and redeem it. When you realize that His provision is a done deal, you can lay hold to the eternity and power within you. You can rid yourself of contrary temporal thoughts and cast down the imaginations that were set against us. Since the devil was already openly defeated and his dominion has long been over, we are all learning to eliminate every oppo-sition within ourselves to receive our promised inheritance.

We will move into the realm of healings that require time, and into miracles that have no respect for the time of the world. We will move into a realm of creative miracles that can grow body parts and limbs as quickly as Eve grew from a rib and dismiss diseases as immediately as Jesus speaking away leprosy.

"The life was manifested, and we have seen, and bear witness, and declare to you that eternal life which was with the Father and was manifested to us" 1 John 1:2 NKJ

"...Jesus answered and said to him, "If anyone loves Me, he will keep My word; and My Father will love him, and We will come to him and make Our home with him." John 14:23 NKJ

"See then that ye walk circumspectly, not as fools, but as wise, Redeeming the time, because the days are evil. Wherefore be ye not unwise, but understanding what the will of the Lord is." Ephesians 5:15-17

"And as soon as he had spoken, immediately the leprosy departed from him, and he was cleansed." Mark 1:42

The enemy has used old tactics to lengthen the *appeal* on a certain death sentence. He also tries to get in the way of his removal from people to dry places. If he can get the body of Christ to be *delayed, wait* or *procrastinate* for prayer, preaching, saving souls and other moves of the Spirit, it will buy him time. He knows you have authority over him, but if he can get you to *think twice* about it and *linger* on his convincing thoughts, you will lose ground and have to make up the time in meditation of the Word. When you learn to move at the speed of God, you learn there is no waiting in eternity. When you learn to stay in this realm, your comfort will not cease. When you exercise your spiritual muscles and pray into the yes and Amen of God's promises, your anointing will destroy every yoke. When the 'sleeping giant' body of Christ wakes up and realizes this dominion as a whole, the tiny captivating threads of the adversary will be broken off and a new era will begin.

"Therefore rejoice, O heavens, and you who dwell in them! Woe to the inhabitants of the earth and the sea! For the devil has come down to you, having great wrath, because he knows that he has a short time." Revelation 12:12 NKJ

"Because you have made the LORD, who is my refuge, even the most High, your dwelling place, No evil shall befall you, nor shall any plague come near your dwelling." Psalm 91:9, 10 NKJ

"For all the promises of God in him are yea, and in him Amen, unto the glory of God by us." 2 Corinth-ians 1:20

The bible shows us over time man's growth from the revelation of God. In modern science, our accelerated learning tells us that we won't know 75% of what we will know 25 years from now. In the curve of God's acceleration, knowledge will exponentially increase even more. The seeds He has planted will make an everlasting harvest. The time that we've lost in the past are being renewed in fields of men embracing the Seed and coming into the intimacy with Christ. We will receive as much as we can handle.

In the bible; Cain had much to learn about anger and sacrificing. Noah found the grace of God. Abraham was a friend of God. Moses brought the initial engagement of God's cooperate promise to the children of Israel. King David ushered in praise and worship. Jesus taught dominion with performance. Now, the Holy Spirit guides us and shows us the future. We are all rewarded in growth with personal revelation when we seek after Him in faith.

"...and He will tell you things to come." John 16:13 NKJ

"...he is a rewarder of them that diligently seek him." Hebrews 11:6

God wants to penetrate the earth with His Spirit. As the Father looks at time *as we would look at a clock* and see all events at once, He sees and rewards those who place their selves in a position to walk in His ever available Spirit. Since He has validated us, we are chosen to subdue the earth with His extremely capable presence. Although we were designed to be immortal, we lost our dominion over time when Adam stepped into the time realm after sin. As the clock of time started for us, the condemnation of temporary teaching of the world system began dealing an everlasting death sentence for those who chose to walk in what the temporal world had to offer. In the redemption that was more powerful than anything the curse put against us, we can receive the truth that will make us free and can walk into dominion over time. When you become aware of the essence of His timelessness, your identification of this connection becomes personal impartation and physical manifestation to the world you are guided to change and the life God has always called you to walk in with an unwavering expectancy of dominion.

"...Your kingdom come. Your will be done, as in heaven, so in earth." Luke 11:2 NKJ

"If we live in the Spirit, let us also walk in the Spirit." Galatians 5:25

"For I know the thoughts that I think toward you, says the LORD, thoughts of peace and not of evil, to give you a future and a hope. Then you will call upon Me and go and pray to Me, and I will listen to you. And you will seek Me and find *Me,* when you search for Me with all your heart. I will be found by you, says the LORD, and I will bring you back from your captivity; I will gather you from all the nations and from all the places where I have driven you, says the LORD, and I will bring you to the place from which I cause you to be carried away captive." Jeremiah 29:11-14 NKJ

God has chosen you from the foundation of the world and called you a doer of the Word before you did anything. You would be defaulted in a world of deceit if you chose not to respond to God's Word. Your response has guided you into personal time with Him and brought into places with access to chosen teachers and ministers as you search Him out. The Word is a mirror of all you can be. You should not see who God says you are in the Word and then forget it by weighing things out with temporary circumstances. Keep a viewpoint from the eyes of God and hold unto His vision.

"Just as He chose us in Him before the foundation of the world, that we should be holy and without blame before Him in love, having predestined us to adoption as sons by Jesus Christ to Himself, according to the good pleasure of His will" Ephesians 1:4, 5 NKJ

"Moreover whom he did predestinate, them he also called: and whom he called, them he also justified: and whom he justified, them he also glorified." Romans 8:30

"But as many as received him, to them gave he power to become the sons of God, even to them that believe on his name: **Which were born, not of blood, nor of the will of the flesh, nor of the will of man, but of God."** **John 1:12, 13**

"Don't fool yourself into thinking that you are a lis-tener when you are anything but, letting the Word go in one ear and out the other. Act on what you hear! Those who hear and don't act are like those who glance in the mirror, walk away, and two minutes later have no idea who they are, what they look like." James 1:22-24 MB

Our confidence rises with the belief in our innocence. Since forgiveness is a place in eternity, we can always boldly come to the throne of grace. Because God is love, He does not decide *if* to forgive, but it is a description of His unchanging nature. We can immediately know there is powerful and merciful grace available in forgiveness for the *'worst'* of sin, especially since the temporal and corrupt things are not living in God, being separated as far as the east is from the west. Only the everlasting living things such as prayer continue living in the eternity you are welcome to anytime. In that secret heavenly place with Jesus, you are not conscious of sin, but power and absolute victory.

You can stay walking in His eternal Spirit by forgiving yourself and being forgiving to others. Your perspective of seeing yourself and others without blemish as God does; eliminates *unrighteous judgment, comparisons* and *superiority complexes.* When you have a thought pattern with no respecter of persons, you will not interrupt the time flow of giving or receiving of previously granted miracles.

"And friends, once that's taken care of and we're no longer accusing or condemning ourselves, we're bold and free before God! We're able to stretch our hands out and

receive what we asked for because we're doing what he said, doing what pleases him." 1 John 3:21, 22 MB

"Assuredly, I say to you, all sins will be forgiven the sons of men, and whatever blasphemies they may utter" Mark 3:28 NKJ

"And when they were come to the place, which is called Calvary, there they crucified him, and the malefactors, one on the right hand, and the other on the left. Then said Jesus, Father, forgive them; for they know not what they do...." Luke 23:33, 34

"At my first answer no man stood with me, but all men forsook me: I pray God that it may not be laid to their charge." 2 Timothy 4:16

"And whenever you stand praying, if you have anything against anyone, forgive him that your Father in heaven may also forgive you your trespasses. But if you do not forgive, neither will your Father in heaven forgive your trespasses" Mark 11:25, 26 NKJ

Since man has fallen short, we become reactive on how the Word moves us. God is not reactive like we would be in giving us an answer or response to prayers and supplications for provision, but His supply is already a done deal. His angels are already instructed to hearken to the voice of God that comes from us. He is not moved by our need, but the name (*or authority*) of the Son is here to 'move mountains' with the cooperation of our mouths inspired by the indwelling within us. Eternity lives in us and must be expressed through us. Our words and confession speak life into existence from what we know is available to us. We choose what we will accelerate. We choose how soon a fig tree withers or a disease fades away.

Our good works will follow us into eternity, because of the source of these works lives in eternity. The Inspiration will not come back empty. Worldly things that will be former, will not come to mind, but people, family and all the creatures that wait upon the manifestation of the people of God, will be with us forever. Even as we enter into His throne room now, sin is not remembered in His presence. There is a great oneness in mind. As God is: Mind (Father), Spirit (Holy Ghost) and Soul (Jesus), our own being is mind, spirit and soul becomes one with Him. The triune being of God is not $1+1+1=3$, but $1 \times 1 \times 1=1$. The more our thoughts conform to our Lord, the more we see as we are known. Our beings are being translated into the oneness and timelessness of His nature.

"...life is in the power of the tongue" Proverbs 18:21

"Jesus sensed that his disciples were having a hard time with this and said, "Does this throw you completely? What would happen if you saw the Son of Man ascending to where he came from? The Spirit can make life. Sheer muscle and willpower don't make anything happen. Every word I've spoken to you is a Spirit-word, and so it is life-making the words that I speak unto you, they are spirit, and they are life." John 6:61-63

"So shall My word be that goes forth from My mouth; It shall not return to Me void, But it shall accomplish what I please, And it shall prosper *in the thing* for which I sent it." Isaiah 53:11 NKJ

"Bless the LORD, ye his angels, that excel in strength, that do his commandments, hearkening unto the voice of his word." Psalm 103:20

"...'Blessed *are* the dead who die in the Lord from now on.'

'Yes,' says the Spirit, 'that they may rest from their labors, and their works follow them.'" Revelation 14:13 NKJ

"For behold, I create new heavens and a new earth; And the former shall not be remembered or come to mind." Isaiah 65:16, 17 NKJ

"I and my Father are one." John 10:30

"For now we see through a glass, darkly; but then face to face: now I know in part; but then shall I know even as also I am known." 1 Corinthians 13:12

We should live in the now with God. Our purpose is to bring the truth, life and power of eternity; into the lives of men in this time. We know that the majority of the God's word is for the time we have in these earthly tabernacles. We won't need healing in our eternal heaven, or open up deaf ears there, but the blood provision has been made to enjoy the abundant life here, while we wait for our change to come and rescue those who are blind, broken hearted and bound. The access to eternity is for now and the leaves of the tree of life are here to heal the nations are for now. The Word has very few limits on what is available now. The throne of grace is available for any situation and invites us in a continual communion with God at all times.

"Let us hear the conclusion of the whole matter: Fear God, and keep his commandments: for this is the whole duty of man." Ecclesiastes 12:13

"And Jesus came and spoke to them, saying, "All authority has been given to Me in heaven and on earth. Go therefore and make disciples of all the nations, baptizing them in the name of the Father and of the Son and of the Holy Spirit, teaching them to observe all things that I have commanded you; and lo, I am with you always, even to the end of the age." Matthew 28:19, 20 NKJ

"...and the leaves of the tree were for the healing of the nations." Revelation 22:2

As heirs of Christ, the present and future manifestations of time belong to us. We inherit all as a family in Christ. We have a title deed in faith of what is permanently ours. When we take our mind off the temporal circumstances of the world in front of us, we will keep our divine appointments. God wants to use the power invested in us to bring glory to His kingdom;

"Therefore let no man glory in men. For all things are yours... life, or death, or things present, or things to come; all are yours" 1 Corinthians 3:22

"So if you're serious about living this new resurrection life with Christ, act like it. Pursue the things over which Christ presides. Don't shuffle along, eyes to the ground, absorbed with the things right in front of you. Look up, and be alert to what is going on around Christ-that's where the action is..." Colossians 3:1, 2 MB

We have a natural born tendency as man, to sub-consciously know the there is a way to see into the future. In our spirit, we know that there's something or someone out there who knows (*that's why palm-readers and horo-scopes make a lot of money by attempting to fulfill this desire*). However, the Spirit within us is poured out on **all** flesh. Without the revelation that there's a Guide to lead us, we have natural tendencies to look into the future at the '*other reports*' carefully woven and spoken to direct you into failure.

Men of God who lived above the restrictions of the natural laws traveled through time and space (Acts 8:39, 40), spoke and time went backwards (2 Kings 20:11) or spoke and time stood still (Joshua 10:12, 13). And that's just a few that we've heard about, besides Jesus getting into the boat three or four miles away from the shore and immediately arriving there. Time or speed is not an issue in the Spirit when eter-nity is dominating the event. When we need to accomplish divine appointments this dominion is ever present.

"But this is that which was spoken by the prophet Joel; And it shall come to pass in the last days, saith God, I will pour out of my Spirit upon all flesh..." Acts 2:16, 17

"So when they had rowed about three or four miles, they saw Jesus walking on the sea and drawing near the boat; and they were afraid. But He said to them, 'It is I; do not be afraid.' Then they willingly received Him into the boat, and immediately the boat was at the land where they were going." John 6:19-21 NKJ

People may talk a lot about how Jesus is coming back and you should be ready, which is true physically, but Jesus wants to come back to give you a Now word, or what is called a *rhema* (living) word. Be ready if you get a call and somebody tells you they're dying. You don't want to have to get 'prayed up' and get back to them. Keep your eyes on eternity and pray without ceasing. Stay prepared. You want to remain consistent and be able tell anyone; 'Don't worry about it, I'm going to pray'.

"Moreover as for me, God forbid that I should sin against the LORD in ceasing to pray for you..." 1 Samuel 12:23

"Pray all the time." 1 Thessalonians 5:17 MB

"Praying always with all prayer and supplication in the Spirit, and watching thereunto with all perseverance and supplication for all saints" Ephesians 6:18

We were designed to live in one time realm. True life is always in the now... It's the only time realm that the Spirit breaths in us and inspires us. If we leave this time realm we cease to receive the instructions and authority for the now. Being a slave to the past can bring stagnation, sorrow and sin consciousness. Being a slave to the future can bring anxiety and worry. We can't live in the past or make a mental ascent to the future. Our rhema is not in the past. The rhema is not in the future... it may be for the future, but it is not the future. Our obedience to what God has said in His (*logos*) word opens us up to the living (*rhema*) word. In other words, accepting Jesus as Lord brings us to the current activity of the Holy Spirit we all search for.

The bible is not a history book. It's a book about a living person. God's name is not *I was*, but I Am. We are here to walk in a relationship, not a memory. If your memories are bigger than your dreams, you have lost hope. We need to have daily bread for today (*although stale bread is good for the starving*) to receive direction for now. Again, the Word says; as Jesus IS, so are we in the world. When Zechariah prayed long before the birth of John, the angels said your prayers **are** heard, letting him know his prayer stays in eternity and answered in a divine appointment.

"...for the testimony of Jesus is the spirit of prophecy" Revelation 19:10

"...because as he is, so are we in this world." 1 John 4:17

"But the angel said to him, 'Do not be afraid, Zacharias: for your prayer is heard..." Luke 1:13 NKJ

Don't be satisfied with yesterday's accomplishments, but keep pressing toward the mark of the high calling of God. Recognize what makes you weak and resist it. Get a promise on your deliverance in the Word and meditate on it until you don't waiver anymore. If you waiver, you lose your sense of power, anointing and authority. Continue to quicken your spiritual reflexes. When you flow with Him you can count on a greater power than you have yourself to come upon you when someone needs it.

Your yesterday may have lied to you, your Sunday school teacher may have ignorantly misinformed you, but God hasn't placed these limits on the churches, the churches have placed these limits on God. You have all the potential to realize you are who the bible says you are. You cannot prosper much by somebody else's experience, if it falls short of New Testament experience. If you do, you may receive the same thing the enemy has given them. The sooner you crucify the old-man, the better off you'll be. The 'old man' is useless to you and cannot comprehend where you are or where you're going. When you let go of everything you have, you receive everything that Jesus has. Your faith will accept the pre-view by perceiving what isn't and speak it into a now realm. Again, there was never anointing or power that Jesus claimed that was for Him and not for us. We are co-laborers. We plant seeds and God puts His no limit 'miracle grow' on it.

"I do not pray for these alone, but also for those who will believe in Me through their word; that they all may be one, as You, Father, *are* in Me, and I in You; that they also may be one in Us, that the world may believe that You sent Me. And the glory which You gave Me I have given them, that they may be one just as We are one: I in them, and You in Me; that they may be made perfect in one, and that the world may know that You have sent Me, and have loved them as You have loved Me." John 17:20-23 NKJ

The dominion over time will fill a basket of fish, before you can empty it. It will multiply oil faster than you can pour it out. The God of abundance and multiplication will have you bypass time and accomplish His work.

Jesus always talked in faith like things were already a done deal, because it really is. His words appeared to weave in and out of our time realm;

"I have glorified You on the earth. I have finished the work which You have given Me to do. And now, O Father, glorify Me together with Yourself, with the glory which I had with You before the world was." John 17:4, 5 NKJ

"Now I am no longer in the world, but these are in the world, and I come to You. Holy Father, keep through Your name those whom You have given Me, that they may be one as We *are*. While I was with them in the world, I kept them in Your name. Those whom You gave Me I have kept; and none of them is lost except the son of perdition, that the Scripture might be fulfilled." John 17:11, 12 NKJ

"Now is the judgment of this world: now shall the prince of this world be cast out." John 12:31

When you see things from the Fathers realm, your faith will tell on you by your confession. Your words are here to carry the everlasting Presence and events in them. You can let the mind which was also in Christ Jesus, also be in you and walk by 'now' faith and not by sight. You can relate to our Father better when you think of Him as a constant unchanging living being and realize our connection with Him allows us to flow with Him in the face of eternity.

"You search the Scriptures, for in them you think you have eternal life; and these are they which testify of Me." John 5:39 NKJ

"that whoever believes in Him should not perish but have eternal life." John 3:15 NKJ

"My sheep hear my voice, and I know them, and they follow me: And I give unto them eternal life; and they shall never perish, neither shall any man pluck them out of my hand." John 10:26, 27

"And this is eternal life, that they may know You, the only true God, and Jesus Christ whom You have sent." John 17:3 NKJ

CHAPTER 8

Dominion Over Darkness

A ll of the great separations of the bible in the dispensa-tions of time are pre-measured. No amount of dark-ness can take a permanent stand against light. Every event that darkness produces will be swallowed up in defeat. From the separation of light and darkness, day and night, corrupt angels, the tree of life from man, the exodus from Egypt, the Amorites, the 'divorce' of Israel (Jer. 3:8) and until the full-ness of times and ultimately the lake of fire, light overcomes darkness. Even as light is measured at around 300,000 kilo-meters per second, the unstoppable, undeniable power of God's Light multiplies much faster than darkness and will exceed every corner of the universe. This Light is our illu-mination of knowledge and understanding.

"And the light shines in the darkness, and the darkness did not comprehend it." John 1:5 NKJ

"So the great dragon was cast out, that serpent of old, called the Devil and Satan, who deceives the whole world; he was cast to the earth, and his angels were cast out with him." Revelation 12:9 NKJ

"So he drove out the man; and he placed at the east of the garden of Eden Cherubims, and a flaming sword which turned every way, to keep the way of the tree of life." Genesis 3:24

"Then He said to Abram: 'Know certainly that your descendants will be strangers in a land *that is* not theirs, and will serve them, and they will afflict them four hundred years. And also the nation whom they serve I will judge; afterward they shall come out with great possessions.'" Genesis 15:13, 14 NKJ

"But in the fourth generation they shall return here, for the iniquity of the Amorites *is* not yet complete." Genesis 15:16 NKJ

"having made known to us the mystery of His will, according to His good pleasure which He purposed in Himself, that in the dispensation of the fullness of the times He might gather together in one all things in Christ, both which are in heaven and which are on earth—in Him" Ephesians 1:9, 10 NKJ

As a prophet, the most powerful thing that Jesus did was to get people to trust in the living God. He made the believers to believe and preached what He wanted them to believe in. They could not do it with their own understanding or get revelation from their leaders. He taught people how to follow God. He brought light into darkness.

"Trust in the LORD with all your heart; and lean not on your own understanding." Proverbs 3:5 NKJ

"In him was life; and the life was the light of men." John 1:4

What you know will become your life. What you teach will become your harvest. If you have not died to self, you have very little to offer. When you get a 'fix' from God it will addict you away from what the world has to offer.

As you progress to become a greater light in the world, the unseen world will become aware of the brightness that you allow God to flow through you. And even as one angel lighted up the earth (Rev. 18:1), you can accelerate your potential to be brighter with the Treasure you have within you. When the Son is manifested through the kings of the united body of Christ, there will be no need for any other natural light.

"You are the light of the world. A city that is set on a hill cannot be hidden. Nor do they light a lamp and put it under a basket, but on a lampstand, and it gives light to all *who are* in the house. Let your light so shine before men, that they may see your good works and glorify your Father in heaven." Matthew 5:14-16 NKJ

"And I saw another mighty angel come down from heaven, clothed with a cloud: and a rainbow was upon his head, and his face was as it were the sun..." Revelation 10:1

"For it is the God who commanded light to shine out of darkness, who has shone in our hearts to *give* the light of the knowledge of the glory of God in the face of Jesus Christ. But we have this treasure in earthen vessels, that the excellence of the power may be of God and not of us." 2 Corinthians 4:6, 7 NKJ

"And has made us kings and priests His God and Father..." Revelation 1:6 NKJ

"The city had no need of the sun or of the moon to shine in it, for the glory of God illuminated it. The Lamb *is* its light. And the nations of those who are saved shall walk in its light, and the kings of the earth bring their glory and honor into it." Revelation 21:23, 24 NKJ

"Then shall the righteous shine forth as the sun in the kingdom of their Father. Who hath ears to hear, let him hear." Matthew 13:43

Our relationship with God is more about being in His light and direction than it is to cast out demons. We don't have to switch off darkness, just stay in the Light. We don't have to confess what the world or the devil is doing, but what God is doing through us. Our dominion, victory and total domination is in Him. When we exercise our time down to hours, minutes and moments of awareness, we can test to see where our fellowship is spiritually with God.

"Examine yourselves, whether ye be in the faith; prove your own selves..." 2 Corinthians 13:5

A spirit has a breath, or a voice that plants seeds. Inside you, there are or has been many existing and deep rooted. Good seeds are planted by the Holy Spirit and *bad seeds* or *weeds*, are planted by the tempter. Some plants or weeds from the enemy are easy to pick. Bad roots will grow deep, until the understanding of the Word takes dominion over it. When you fertilize the ground, weeds will also thrive. That's why a bad seed may get stronger with certain scriptures or certain ministers who don't handle the Word well. *The food may be good but the cook has dirty hands.* The bad seed had been validated by what looked to be a good caretaker, but was a wolf that didn't care for the sheep. The hired person who's in it for the money will not regard your spiritual life a priority. When prayers are made and someone comes to intercede, what has not been a harvest will have increase.

"but while men slept, his enemy came and sowed tares among the wheat and went his way. But when the grain had sprouted and produced a crop, then the tares also appeared. So the servants of the owner came and said to him, 'Sir, did you not sow good seed in your field? How then does it have tares?' He said to them, 'An enemy has done this.'..." Matthew 13:25-28 NKJ

"...we faint not; But have renounced the hidden things of dishonesty, not walking in craftiness, nor handling the word of God deceitfully; but by manifestation of the truth commending ourselves to every man's conscience in the sight of God." 2 Corinthians 4:1, 2

"But a hireling, *he who is* not the shepherd, one who does not own the sheep, sees the wolf coming and leaves the sheep and flees; and the wolf catches the sheep and scatters them." John 10:12 NKJ

"Then he said to the keeper of his vineyard, 'Look, for three years I have come seeking fruit on this fig tree and find none. Cut it down; why does it use up the ground?' But he answered and said to him, 'Sir, let it alone this year also, until I dig around it and fertilize *it*. And if it bears fruit, *well*. But if not, after that you can cut it down.'" Luke 13:7-9 NKJ

When God said "Let there be light" this dominion over darkness relates to the dominion over time because light involves time. This was a foresight to the dominion we would need to have with the Word that was manifested from the beginning. The Light of the world said that we are the light of the world. As Satan fell like lightning from heaven, our dominion over darkness in the spiritual world is what makes demons run at the speed of light. The word is near thee, even in your mouth. When you know your 'ABCs', or the assurance, boldness and confidence in the Word; those defeated spirits, who try to delay your progress, will run away faster. The anointed words of a believer travel at the speed of God. At the speed of God you can pray on one side of the world, and in an instant, have it travel to the other side. You could be on a space shuttle around the moon and have the prayers of the righteous reach out to you, at the speed of God.

"And God said, Let there be light: and there was light. And God saw the light, that it was good: and God divided the light from the darkness." Genesis 1:3, 4

"There was a man sent from God, whose name was John. The same came for a witness, to bear witness of the Light, that all men through him might believe... That was the true Light..." John 1:6-9

"Jesus said, "I know. I saw Satan fall, a bolt of lightning out of the sky."" Luke 10:18 MB

"The word that saves is right here, as near as the tongue in your mouth, as close as the heart in your chest." Romans 10:8 MB

Your dominion over the earth and all that has been recovered from what the enemy has stolen will have you realize that you have victory whether it is mosquitoes or mountain lions. When you know that God wants you to not only have the blessing of Abraham, but the blessing of Adam before his fall, the victory becomes a giant and the problems become like grasshoppers. Don't let the devil talk to you and give you a cold symptom, *'you're tired'*, *'lay down and relax'*, *'get some medication'* without getting direction from God on what to think and what to do. Don't let an opinionated doctor or lawyer give you a death sentence without talking to the One who can heal you or bring you out of jail. For any bad reports you receive, at the very least you should began to pray for the body of Christ for the specific attack of the adversary. In other words if you feel a pain in your body and you know it's not yours, you may be feeling an attack on another member of the body of Christ, so pray and intercede against it until it flees. You know what the end is going to be for you and your enemies. If they tell you about your (*false*) future, tell them about their true future (*even if you have to pray under your breath in a crowd*). When the demons asked if they would be tortured before their time, it indicated the possibility of it happening. Your Spirit led words are torture. Your dominion reigns over darkness.

"... and let them have dominion...over all the earth..."
Genesis 1:26

"God created human beings; he created them godlike, reflecting God's nature. He created them male and female. God blessed them: "Prosper! Reproduce! Fill Earth! Take charge!" Genesis 1:27, 28 MB

"...and nothing shall by any means hurt you." Luke 10:19

"My God sent His angel and shut the lions' mouths, so that they have not hurt me..." Daniel 6:22 NKJ

"...He will be very gracious to you at the sound of your cry; When He hears it, He will answer you...Your ears shall hear a word behind you, saying, This *is* the way,

walk in it," Whenever you turn to the right hand or whenever you turn to the left." Isaiah 30:19, 21 NKJ

"And suddenly they cried out, saying, 'What have we to do with You, Jesus, You Son of God? Have You come here to torment us before the time?'" Matthew 8:29 NKJ

"You believe that there is one God. You do well. Even the demons believe—and tremble!" James 2:19 NKJ

"And the devil that deceived them was cast into the lake of fire and brimstone, where the beast and the false prophet are, and shall be tormented day and night for ever and ever." Revelation 20:10

"All who knew you among the peoples are astonished at you; You have become a horror, And *shall be* no more forever." Ezekiel 28:19 NKJ

CHAPTER 9

Dominion Over Distance

S ome say a picture is worth a thousand words. The bigger view that we see of a picture can make the details of it look very small. In our lives, if we take a five year view of things and compare those to a view point of one day, many daily details seem less significant. When we look at life from an eternal point of view, our natural plans diminish in the sight of God. In the Father, there is no relevancy in time, distance or size. The Spirit of God is the connection through our portal of time and elements. The Spirit or voice of God has an origin from eternity. Thus painting a spiritual picture of the pathway to God is done by the Word. The Word who made all things (John 14:6, 1:12, Col 1:15), is the written expression of eternal life. These words are still alive today, connecting to our spirit. Wisdom is the attachment to this destiny of life and soul preservation. Using living words, this chapter will paint a picture of these expressions.

God is not only bigger than big, but He made both great and small and cannot be contained;

"But will God indeed dwell on the earth? Behold, heaven and the heaven of heavens cannot contain You. How much less this temple which I have built?" 1 Kings 8:27

There is no place where his Spirit does not reach;

"Where can I go from Your Spirit? Or where can I flee from Your presence? If I ascend into heaven, You *are* there; If I make my bed in hell, behold, You *are there*. If I take the wings of the morning, *And* dwell in the uttermost parts of the sea, Even there Your hand shall lead me, And Your right hand shall hold me." Psalm 139:7-10 NKJ

The Omni-present God of the universe created the ever expanding universe. The star in our solar system which we call the sun is 960,000 times the size of our planet. Or, as Lou Giglio puts it, if the earth was the size of a golf ball, it would be enough golf balls to fill up a school bus to equal the size of the sun. A bigger star is Beltegese. It would be 263 billion times the size of the earth. It is twice the size of earth's orbit around the sun. An even bigger star is Canis Majoris. It would take 7 quadrillion earths to make up this star, or enough 'golf balls' to fill up the entire state of Texas... 22 inches deep. Yet God is the Creator of every star in every galaxy, who has named and directed each star.

"He sees the number of the stars; he gives them all their names." Psalm 147:4

The stars give shine and give Him glory;

"Praise ye him, sun and moon: praise him, all ye stars of light." Psalm 148:3

And He hides them from giving light during judgment, the day of the Lord when He will have vengeance on the enemies of His people and folds them up and throw them away like old cothes;

"When *I* put out your light, I will cover the heavens, and make its stars dark; I will cover the sun with a cloud, and the moon shall not give her light." Ezekiel 32:7 NKJ

"Behold, the day of the LORD comes, cruel, with both wrath and fierce anger, to lay the land desolate; and He will destroy its sinners from it. For the stars of heaven and their constellations will not give their light; the sun will be darkened in its going forth, and the moon will not cause its light to shine." Isaiah 13:9, 10 NKJ

"In the beginning, Lord, you laid the foundation of the earth and made the heavens with your hands. You will fold them up like a cloak and discard them like old clothing." Hebrews 1:10, 12 NLT

The sun, moon and stars were not only created for days and years, but also for signs;

"And God said, Let there be lights in the firmament of the heaven to divide the day from the night; and let them be for signs, and for seasons, and for days, and years" Genesis 1:14

"And God made two great lights; the greater light to rule the day, and the lesser light to rule the night: he made the stars also." Genesis 1:16

"And there shall be signs in the sun, and in the moon, and in the stars..." Luke 21:25

The stars have God given names and tell the story in the universe above us from many miles away. The constellations of the zodiac (*Hebrew; Mazzaroth* see Job 38:32 *Sanskrit the root'zoad' means a way or path*) were clearly known from the beginning. In the oldest stories about the stars in earth's history, they showed 12 chapters of a story beginning with the virgin with seed (*Virgo; Hebrew 'Bethulah'*) to the triumph of God long before men got a hold of it (Is 47:13). Ungodly men using our desire for guidance and expectations (*that we should get from the Holy Spirit*) and their desire for gain twisted the stories of these signs to fit their own desires;

"...Where are all your astrologers, those stargazers who make predictions each month? Let them stand up and save you from what the future holds. But they are like straw burning in a fire; they cannot save themselves from the flame. You will get no help from them at all; their hearth is no place to sit for warmth." Is 47:13, 14 NLT

These stories are captured in the events of the written word. For example, the 'chapter' of Libra (*Hebrew 'Mozanaim' or scales* see Dan 5:27) refers to the redemption of God. In this celestial section; the Northern Crown or *'Cornone Borealis'* shines at midnight every night over the city of Jerusalem (Matt 2:2,9). The Southern Cross or *'Crux'* constellation (*visible during different centuries*) with the Messiah's 'star' disappeared (Dan 9:26) at almost the exact time when Jesus was on the cross (Matt 27:35). It was not seen again until the 16th century by sailors traveling the Cape of South Africa. Historians were greatly moved by the reappearance of this constellation after more than a millennium.

"He rescues and saves his people; he performs miraculous signs and wonders in the heavens and on earth..." Daniel 6:27 NLT

The North Star or 'Polaris' the Pole Star *(Greek 'Cynosure' or center of attention)* is the star in heaven upon which our entire heavens now seem to turn. About 6,000 years ago after the fall of Adam and Eve, according to the constant movement of the equinoxes, the pole star used to be 'Draconis', the main star in the constellation of 'Draco' the dragon (Rev 12:9). Currently it is Ursa Minor *(originally referring to the gathering of His people and now as the bear)*. The stars continue today, to tell the stories of the pathway of destiny.

"The heavens proclaim the glory of God. The skies display his craftsmanship. Day after day they continue to speak; night after night they make him known. They speak without a sound or word; their voice is never heard. Yet their message has gone throughout the earth, and their words to all the world." Psalm 19:1-4 NLT

We don't have to worship the stars, as sinners do with things like music, pentagrams and hexagrams, but realize that they are under a God given authority under us, just as Joshua told the star in our solar system to stand still (Joshua 10:12).

In time, I have realized in the my own distant dreamland, I've established dominion in this realm by being aware of my surrounding and exercising control during my sleep. Even if I rise after an unfavorable dream I will go back in and change the circumstances in this domain also. This is another realm that God has made for us and can even talk to us in them. It has been seen in the bible for blessing or warning;

"But God came to Abimelech in a dream by night, and said to him…" Genesis 20:3

"And God came to Laban the Syrian in a dream by night, and said…" Genesis 31:24

"At Gibeon the LORD appeared to Solomon in a dream by night; and God said, 'Ask! What shall I give you?'" 1 Kings 3:5 NKJ

"And being warned of God in a dream that they should not return to Herod, they departed into their own country another way." Matthew 2:12

"And it shall come to pass afterward, that I will pour out my spirit upon all flesh; and your sons and your daughters shall prophesy, your old men shall dream dreams, your young men shall see visions" Joel 2:28

"...If there be a prophet among you, I the LORD will make myself known unto him in a vision, and will speak unto him in a dream." Numbers 12:6

We find in the word that our voices are more powerful then sight. Our utterance is more powerful than observation. If there's a problem you can conquer it, or it will conquer you. You have to examine yourself. Are you natural or supernatural? Are you only human or do you realize you are God filled?

"But as it is written: "Eye has not seen, nor ear heard, Nor have entered into the heart of man the things which God has prepared for those who love Him." But God has revealed them to us through His Spirit...Now we have received, not the spirit of the world, but the Spirit who is from God, that we might know the things that have been freely given to us by God...But the natural man does not receive the things of the Spirit of God, for they are foolishness to him; nor can he know them, because they are spiritually discerned. But he who is spiritual judges all things, yet he himself is rightly judged by no one. For "who has known the mind of the LORD that he may instruct Him?" But we have the mind of Christ." 1 Corinthians 2:9-16 NKJ

In your dominion over distance, there is no size, length or breath in the spirit, just an attachment to the vine of God. Whether we steal a paper clip from the job or rob a bank, that action breaks us away from the fellowship and nourishment of the Vine. Any time we are drawn away, we miss the mark of being a fruitful branch to being unconnected. But, where is heaven but a place connected only to the Spirit? After the end of this age, the universe will all be heavenly places without an adversary. Our ability to have eternal life abiding in us now gives us a place where the enemy cannot reach us, and there is no remembrance of sin.

"For whosoever shall keep the whole law, and yet offend in one point, he is guilty of all." James 2:10

"If a man abide not in me, he is cast forth as a branch, and is withered; and men gather them, and cast them into the fire, and they are burned. If ye abide in me, and my words abide in you, ye shall ask what ye will, and it shall be done unto you." John 15:6, 7

Our spirit is not measurable, whether we are an embryo, or a full grown adult. It is designated to be temporarily attached to the dust of the earth to give it life, until it goes back to the God who gave it. If there is an illegal demonic possession of it, we who are attached to the Vine have been commanded to cast the devils out. Jesus bought back the rights of this planet with His blood. He has sealed up the spirit of his people with a connection that is nigh us. Even in our heart. The ability to go boldly to the throne and sit in heavenly places with Him has been granted. God is more permanent in our spirit and more real than the eyes you're reading this book with.

"Then shall the dust return to the earth as it was: and the spirit shall return unto God who gave it." Ecclesiastes 12:7

"Tell them that the kingdom is here. Bring health to the sick. Raise the dead. Touch the untouchables. Kick out the demons. You have been treated generously, so live generously." Matthew 10:8 MB

"The message is very close at hand; it is on your lips and in your heart." And that message is the very message about faith that we preach" Romans 10:8 NLT

In our fleshly bodies, we perceive light as necessary illumination to the things in this world. There may also be times when we get in touch with our spiritual senses, like when we 'feel' someone is looking at us. In the spiritual realm away from our bodies, we perceive light, people and actions unlimited to the flesh we are in now, like the rich man speaking to Abraham, a man he never met. There are also times where the Lord illuminated someone to see with 'spiritual' eyes when prayer was made. Of course, you can also speak God's living Word for someone to be saved and enter into His marvelous light.

"And in hell he lift up his eyes, being in torments, and seeth Abraham afar off, and Lazarus in his bosom. And he cried and said, Father Abraham, have mercy on me, and send Lazarus, that he may dip the tip of his finger in water, and cool my tongue; for I am tormented in this flame." Luke 16:23, 24

"And he answered, Fear not: for they that be with us are more than they that be with them. And Elisha prayed, and said, LORD, I pray thee, open his eyes, that he may see. And the LORD opened the eyes of the young man; and he saw: and, behold, the mountain was full of horses and chariots of fire round about Elisha." 2 Kings 6:17

God doesn't need natural this light for his personal perception;

"Even the darkness hides nothing from You, but the night shines as the day; the darkness and the light are both alike to You" Psalm 139:12 NKJ

The Word tells us the face of His children will shine like the sun (Matt 13:43) at the end of the world, and we will be like Him (1John 3:2) and know even as we are known (1 Cor 13:12). Some will even shine like the stars in heaven (Dan 12:3). Then our glory will be majestically reflected in the heavenly streets of glass like gold (Rev 21:21). There will be no need of the sun there, for we will have the perception needed from God for anything we need to do;

"And the city has no need of the sun nor of the moon to give light to it, for the splendor and radiance (glory) of God illuminate it, and the Lamb is its lamp." Revelation 21:23 AMP

These are things that we have seen pre-views of at the mount of transfiguration. Moses and Elijah dominated distance and met Jesus, whose face shined like the sun. Even an angel illuminated the earth;

"Now after six days Jesus took Peter, James, and John his brother, led them up on a high mountain by themselves;

and He was transfigured before them. His face shone like the sun, and His clothes became as white as the light. And behold, Moses and Elijah appeared to them, talking with Him." Matthew 17:1-3 NKJ

"And after these things I saw another angel come down from heaven, having great power; and the earth was lightened with his glory." Revelation 18:1

In your connection to eternity, this reflection of distance shows the keys of dominion over distance. God is not the *'man upstairs'* or an *'up there'* God but a here and now God. When you eliminate the barriers of distance, the indwelling in you leads your mind and body to conquering distance. God will raise up the champion that is already in you. When you realize the power of the indwelling of God in you, who involves you as a co-worker to replenish the earth and yourself, you have more expectancy in your prayer power on any place on the planet. God wants us to illuminate the universe, but we first have to win by replenishing this planet or realizing how defeated the enemy is and simply pick up the spoils;

"For we are God's fellow workers; you are God's field, *you are* God's building." 1 Corinthians 3:9 NKJ

"But when a stronger than he comes upon him and overcomes him, he takes from him all his armor in which he trusted, and divides his spoils." Luke 11:22 NKJ

You are strategically placed in the body of Christ to control the atmosphere around you. When you are faithful over little, you become faithful over much. Your progression will increase in your environment. You start in your own life. You control your flesh, mind, will and emotions. You speak blessings over your body. What lives under the microscope, you will command to leave under the mighty authority of Jesus name. What forms on your body will bow the knee to the living Word in you. You will instruct your children. You won't let a associate, brother or co-worker get away with planting '*seeds*' in the atmosphere that you are required to dominate in. If you agree to disagree they will at least know where you stand.

"His lord said to him, 'Well *done,* good and faithful servant; you have been faithful over a few things, I will make you ruler over many things..." Matthew 25:23 NKJ

"Assuredly, I say to you, whatever you bind on earth will be bound in heaven, and whatever you shall loose on earth will be loosed in heaven." Matthew 18:18 NKJ

"Wherefore take unto you the whole armour of God, that ye may be able to withstand in the evil day, and having done all, to stand." Ephesians 6:13

In prayer, we move up in intercession for our neighborhood, cities and countries, opening up to global victories in the spirit, and manifestations in the natural. Angels listen and back us up with performance. All the limitations will fall before your feet. You know the delegated authority you have. The mountain will not be moved until someone like YOU speaks to it. It doesn't matter how long it's been there. Because your NAME is written in heaven, you have the kingdom rule within you. Place a demand on the divine deposit that already speaks within you. Even gravity may be active, but a greater one lives in you. When you began to realize the water-walking potential you have over gravity, even your travel will not be restricted. Your natural rule is your acceptance of kingship from believing and receiving.

God is closer than close and his blessing will follow you for the distance of the nations.

"For assuredly, I say to you, whoever says to this mountain, 'Be removed and be cast into the sea,' and does not doubt in his heart, but believes that those things he says will be done, he will have whatever he says." Mark 11:23 NKJ

"And he said, Come. And when Peter was come down out of the ship, he walked on the water, to go to Jesus." Matthew 14:29

"Surely goodness and mercy shall follow me all the days of my life: and I will dwell in the house of the LORD for ever." Psalm 23:6

You are here to deliver what is available to this generation. You don't have to be present to intercede effectively. Even as I have done, you can say the word on a phone answering service and person can receive a miracle. The Word is not bound.

"Jesus said, "I'll come and heal him." "Oh, no," said the captain. "I don't want to put you to all that trouble. Just give the order and my servant will be fine..."" Matthew 8:7, 8 MB

"...the word of God is not bound." 2 Timothy 2:9

Our growth in realizing the eternity that lives within us, will expand in manifestations in our atmosphere. What has been dormant will surely give no place to the devil. Every creature that waits upon the manifestation of the sons of men will rejoice when they see prophecy fulfilled. The world and all that are in it are yours. There are no barriers in distance.

"Neither give place to the devil." Ephesians 4:27 MB

"For the earnest expectation of the creation eagerly waits for the revealing of the sons of God. For we know that the whole creation groans and labors with birth pangs together until now." Romans 8:19, 22 NKJ

"Therefore let no man glory in men. For all things are yours; Whether Paul, or Apollos, or Cephas, or the world, or life, or death, or things present, or things to come; all are yours" 1 Corinthians 3:21, 22

CHAPTER 10

Dominion Over Death

"Heal the sick, cleanse the lepers, raise the dead, cast out devils: freely ye have received, freely give." Matthew 10:8

B elievers know that Jesus is speaking to all of us in this verse. I write this chapter for you to get used to the idea of raising the dead and have the confidence to be ready for the opportunity. The next chapter in your life requires an acceleration of your faith for the people of the world and the body of Christ. Faith is reading God's word and believing it. This is not something that you get a degree in, but you should be aware of the degree that God lives in you. It's just a matter of faith and obedience.

"Why should it be thought a thing incredible with you, that God should raise the dead?" Acts 26:8

You should know that God wants you to do this to give proof of His resurrecting power and to glorify His name. You have the authority to pray for opportunities and be ready to expect miracles to happen. When you have a habitual lifestyle of listening and obeying the Spirit given impressions within you, the direction for resurrection power is more than available. This is a kind of faith that doesn't require the person who has 'fallen asleep' to be taught and preached into belief. This miracle requires your belief. This makes it easier to raise the dead then other miracles. It only requires your faith and obedience. This is the faith that God is putting in you.

"Jesus said to him, "If you can believe, all things *are* possible to him who believes." Mark 9:23 NKJ

You have the same Spirit in you that Jesus walked with. So you can pray that death spirit off of somebody with the indwelling power of God in you. Jesus would not tell you to raise the dead without giving you the power and ability to equip you. You are in the position to speak on God's behalf of what He wants done. So when you seek direction and break into the yes and the Amen of the Spirit, you can use your authority and call that person or lay hands on them and snatch them out of the grave. Jesus didn't tolerate that kind of behavior and neither should you. You can either think like God or think like men.

"Let this same attitude and purpose and [humble] mind be in you, which was in Christ Jesus" Philippians 2:5, 6 AMP

The indwelling of Christ is in you. The equivalency of the image and likeness of God has been placed in you to manifest His will on the planet. When you show up, God shows up. The power of life is on your words. The Presence of God is in your tongue. You can best believe that Jesus got his prayer answered to give us the glory God gave him. His goal is that the world believes God sent His Son. When you lift up Jesus, you will draw all men unto Him.

"And I, if I be lifted up from the earth, will draw all men unto me." John 12:32

We are one in purpose. One thing we realize is that what the thief tried to steal was just a loan that he had to pay back a high interest with. Whatever the devil has borrowed from you, you can best believe that he will restore seven fold. Ultimately, the resurrection of those who are sleep, will rise to meet Christ in the air (1 Thessalonians 4:16). For now, we have the power for our circle of influence to glorify God at least one person at a time. Power over death is another way revealed to us to show how defeated the opposition really is. Not only do we have greater power than death, but *death knows* we have greater power than it. When we take advantage of the opportunity in grace to be *above the law* of sin and death, live with the direction and have a confirmed word from God, we become untouchable like Jesus. The opposition would try to take His life, but he would just walk through them like he was invisible;

"No one takes it from Me, but I lay it down of Myself. I have power to lay it down, and I have power to take it again. This command I have received from My Father." John 10:18 NKJ

"When they heard this, the people in the synagogue were furious. Jumping up, they mobbed him and forced him to the edge of the hill on which the town was built. They intended to push him over the cliff, but he passed right through the crowd and went on his way" Luke 4:28-30 NLT

Your correct acknowledgement will put every enemy under your feet. There will be times when you are led by the Spirit, to see when there is no resistance from others, or led to remove people who are resistant with unbelief to allow the Spirit to move upon you to accomplish the manifestations of His heart. Because you sit in heavenly places to bring heavens' rule down to earth, it is your destiny to give life with the power invested in you.

"For since by man came death, by man came also the resurrection of the dead." 1 Corinthians 15:21

"For as the Father raises the dead and gives life to *them,* even so the Son gives life to whom He will." John 5:21 NKJ

When you received power to become sons of God, and believed in the name, the enemy tried to take away that word so you wouldn't build confidence in it. He tries to use history or '*I'll believe it when I see it*' walk by sight and not by faith mentality. In Job, when the sons of God presented themselves, the adversary was there also. Like a menace in jail, he always wants to '*punk*' you and take away your spiritual food away if you let him;

"And these are the ones by the wayside where the word is sown. When they hear, Satan comes immediately and takes away the word that was sown in their hearts." Mark 4:15 NKJ

But the same Spirit that rebuked the devil through the archangel Michael is in you. We will choose to hold unto our Word of life without wavering because of the meditation of our heart. Things are always thought, spoken and exist. Those of us having the mind of Christ will pray His thoughts and speak them aloud and get Spirit backed results.

"But we continue to preach because we have the same kind of faith the psalmist had when he said, "I believed in God, so I spoke" 2 Corinthians 4:13 NLT

"And we are confident that he hears us whenever we ask for anything that pleases him. And since we know he hears us when we make our requests, we also know that he will give us what we ask for." 1 John 5:14, 15 NLT

Looking at eight times that people have been raised from the dead in the bible, it has been not only a New Testament experience, but an acknowledgment of the power of Godly connections.

"Still, everyone died—from the time of Adam to the time of Moses—even those who did not disobey an explicit commandment of God, as Adam did. Now Adam is a symbol, a representation of Christ, who was yet to come." Romans 5:14 NLT

Moses found out the grave could not hold him. There was a spiritual loophole to be free from death. When the archangel Michael took away the body of Moses it took disabled the temporary reign of death.

"Yet Michael the archangel, in contending with the devil, when he disputed about the body of Moses, dared not bring against him a reviling accusation, but said, "The Lord rebuke you!" Jude 1:9 NKJ

Death was a loser from the beginning. Since the credit check before Calvary found that the lamb was slain before the foundation of the world (Rev 13:8), paying the restorative price of life, ahead of time, there was no hesitation of the part of God's chosen men. Elijah prayed to the Lord for a boy's soul to come back to him.

"And he stretched himself out over the child three times and cried out to the Lord, 'O Lord my God, please let this child's life return to him.' The Lord heard Elijah's prayer, and the life of the child returned, and he revived! Then Elijah brought him down from the upper room and gave him to his mother. 'Look!' he said. 'Your son is alive!'" 1 Kings 17:21-23 NLT

Elisha removed a mother and his servant and made a prayer closet;

"When Elisha arrived, the child was indeed dead, lying there on the prophet's bed. He went in alone and shut the door behind him and prayed to the Lord. Then he lay down on the child's body, placing his mouth on the child's mouth, his eyes on the child's eyes, and his hands on the child's hands. And as he stretched out on him, the child's body began to grow warm again! Elisha got up, walked back and forth across the room once, and then stretched himself out again on the child. This time the boy sneezed seven times and opened his eyes!" 2 Kings 4:32-35 NLT

The Presence that was upon him would bring her son back to life. Even after Elisha died, there was enough virtue in his bones to restore life;

"Once when some Israelites were burying a man, they spied a band of these raiders. So they hastily threw the corpse into the tomb of Elisha and fled. But as soon as the body touched Elisha's bones, the dead man revived and jumped to his feet!" 2 Kings 13:21 NLT

There are times when Jesus had to remove people with unbelief away from the immediate atmosphere of a resurrection. His request was for them to only believe;

"While he was still speaking to her, a messenger arrived from the home of Jairus, the leader of the synagogue. He told him, 'Your daughter is dead. There's no use troubling the Teacher now.' But when Jesus heard what had happened, he said to Jairus, 'Don't be afraid. Just have faith, and she will be healed.' When they arrived at the house, Jesus wouldn't let anyone go in with him except Peter, John, James, and the little girl's father and mother. The house was filled with people weeping and wailing, but he said, 'Stop the weeping! She isn't dead; she's only asleep.' But the crowd laughed at him because they all knew she had died. Then Jesus took her by the hand and said in a loud voice, 'My child, get up!' And at that moment her life returned, and she immediately stood up! Then Jesus told them to give her something to eat." Luke 8:49-55 NLT

For then, even as it is now, we need a certain level of agreement. There were places that Jesus healed all or just a few due to a lack of faith.

"And so he did only a few miracles there because of their unbelief." Matthew 13:58 NLT

In another city, the day after he healed the centurion's servant who had great faith, Peter's mother-in-law and everyone who was brought to him, there were many believers who seen evidence of the power of God and had a certain expectancy. This cooperate level of belief didn't require anyone to be moved. It wasn't the pity or sympathy that lifted him, but the compassion of Jesus;

"Not long after that, Jesus went to the village Nain. His disciples were with him, along with quite a large crowd. As they approached the village gate, they met a funeral procession—a woman's only son was being carried out for burial. And the mother was a widow. When Jesus saw her, his heart broke. He said to her, "Don't cry." Then he went over and touched the coffin. The pallbearers stopped. He said, "Young man, I tell you: Get up." The dead son sat up and began talking. Jesus presented him to his mother." Luke 7:11-15 MB

Jesus needed to raise up the faith of Martha. She believed the last day, or later on resurrection, but not the Present one;

"Now Martha said to Jesus, "Lord, if You had been here, my brother would not have died. But even now I know that whatever You ask of God, God will give You." Jesus said to her, "Your brother will rise again." Martha said to Him, "I know that he will rise again in the resurrection at the last day." Jesus said to her, "I am the resurrection and the life. He who believes in Me, though he may die, he shall live. And whoever lives and believes in Me shall never die. Do you believe this?" John 11:21-26 NKJ

There are times we may need to increase the faith of others by the spoken promises of God's word. For the audience's sake, Jesus told our Father that he heard him, and always will, which gave Martha more faith and insight on what he came to do and the relationship that was available;

"...And Jesus lifted up His eyes and said, "Father, I thank You that You have heard Me. And I know that You always hear Me, but because of the people who are standing by I said this, that they may believe that You sent Me." Now when He had said these things, He cried with a loud voice, "Lazarus, come forth!" And he who had died came out bound hand and foot with graveclothes, and his face was wrapped with a cloth. Jesus said to them, "Loose him, and let him go." John 11:41-44 NKJ

Living with the same indwelling Spirit of God, Peter also had to move people out and make the resurrection a 'done deal' for a disciple;

"Down the road a way in Joppa there was a disciple named Tabitha, "Gazelle" in our language. She was well-known for doing good and helping out. During the time Peter was in the area she became sick and died. Her friends prepared her body for burial and put her in a cool room. Some of the disciples had heard that Peter was visiting in nearby Lydda and sent two men to ask if he would be so kind as to come over. Peter got right up and went with them. They took him into the room where Tabitha's body was laid out. Her old friends, most of them widows, were in the room mourning. They showed Peter pieces of clothing the Gazelle had made while she was with them. Peter put the widows all out of the room. He knelt and prayed. Then he spoke directly to the body: "Tabitha, get up."" Acts 9:36-40 MB

Paul used the resurrection touch to embrace Eutychus (*which means lucky*) after a long sermon and kept preaching till morning;

"We met on Sunday to worship and celebrate the Master's Supper. Paul addressed the congregation. Our plan was to leave first thing in the morning, but Paul talked on, way past midnight. We were meeting in a well-lighted upper room. A young man named Eutychus was sitting in an open window. As Paul went on and on, Eutychus fell sound asleep and toppled out the third-story window. When they picked him up, he was dead. Paul went down, stretched himself on him, and hugged him hard. "No more crying," he said. "There's life in him yet." Then Paul got up and served the Master's Supper. And went on telling stories of the faith until dawn! On that note, they left—Paul going one way, the congregation another, leading the boy off alive, and full of life themselves." Acts 20:7-12 MB

Paul, who knew the peace without the attacks from the enemy was available if he were absent from the body, would rather have resurrected himself to help the cause. After a good stoning, he went on another road trip.

"Then some Jews from Antioch and Iconium caught up with them and turned the fickle crowd against them. They beat Paul unconscious, dragged him outside the town and left him for dead. But as the disciples gathered around him, he came to and got up. He went back into town and the next day left with Barnabas for Derbe." Acts 14:19, 20 MB

"I didn't die. I lived! And now I'm telling the world what God did. God tested me, he pushed me hard, but he didn't hand me over to Death." Psalm 118:17, 18 MB

These miracles are not just for the elite, you are God's elite. God has already given you a green light on the possibilities and put this resurrection power in you. The more you realize the purpose, nature and love of God, the easier these things will come to you without reasoning why you can't. When you see in the spiritual realm the defeat that Jesus gave death on the cross, the vision will empower you to set the captives free. The same power saw many come up out the graves in victory;

"And the graves were opened; and many bodies of the saints which slept arose, And came out of the graves after his resurrection, and went into the holy city, and appeared unto many." Matthew 27:52, 53

The more you believe, the more you receive. The numbers that have passed away in life may seem intimidating, but the Word is greater in you than whatever is in the world. The more you submit, or give your way of thinking to the mindset and will of God; you can resist the temptation of entertaining a second opinion of defeat and get closer to a victorious mindset.

"So humble yourselves before God. Resist the devil, and he will flee from you. Come close to God, and God will come close to you...purify your hearts, for your loyalty is divided between God and the world." James 4:7, 8 NLT

There are many modern day people that God uses for these kinds of miracles. Those of us who have done so, realize a greater power than ourselves came upon them to back up His word with performance. This great anointing is not carried around casually, but is accessible when a need is there and faith is present. Sometimes you may have to remove the skeptics. Sometimes you will release this faith on dead wombs and dead organs. I've even used it on spoiled milk. To a person who knows their God-given authority, death will be like a rat, more scared of you than you are of it.

People look for signs as to what the end is going to be, but when you see the dead being raised on the left and on the right and on the 6:00 news, you better believe that the time is near. This is the time when death will be backed up into a corner, scared of every bible toting, quoting believer. Even after the rapture, death will still run scared, fleeing from anything that looks like the image of God. At that time, Death won't even be taking any volunteers;

"And in those days shall men seek death, and shall not find it; and shall desire to die, and death shall flee from them." Revelation 9:6

In the spiritual realm, the defeat has already happened. The time has come, and now is, that these manifestations of heaven will dominate earth with you playing a vital role in making it happen. Whether you are doing it yourself, or stretching out your hands in faith and agreement with someone else to make it happen, the dominion over death will continue into the restoration of all things. Death does not have the right to go beyond what the Word says.

"O death, where is thy sting? O grave, where is thy victory?" 1 Corinthians 15:55

CHAPTER 11

Great Faith

G reat faith begins at the received word of God. It grows by the Spirit's dwelling on the meditation and your value and honor of it. Faith is a life force, and without it, the Christian life is worthless.

"So then faith *comes* by hearing, and hearing by the word of God." Romans 10:17 NKJ

"For we are God's fellow workers; you are God's field, *you are* God's building." 1 Corinthians 3:7 NKJ

"And if Christ has not been raised, then your faith is useless and you are still guilty of your sins." 1 Corinthians 15:17 NLT

What is believed in your mind will come out of your mouth. Your words will get you closer to a miracle or further away from it. What you say, is more powerful than what you see, when you speak by faith and not by sight. When your words are God inspired, there is greater potential to release power. God is on the throne in the praises that are spoken by any of His people. The angels also listen to the voice of his Word from us. When we believe this, our faith is exercised.

"But You are holy, Enthroned in the praises of Israel." Psalm 22:3 NKJ

"Bless the LORD, you His angels, Who excel in strength, who do His word, Heeding the voice of His word." Psalm 103:20 NKJ

You will always rise to the level of your confession. God will give a promise and you will proclaim it with your conversation. If you continue to confess God's word that says you're healed, you will see the manifestation that you have believed for. When your Faith begins to dominate your confession, you will develop absolute disregard for the circumstances. Your Faith will tell your flesh to "shut up and line up!" Your faith gives you the ability to speak like a King. If you talk about your weakness or powerless Christianity, you will gravitate towards people like you and transfer that same spirit and become overtaken in a fault. You should listen to someone who will challenge you and help you keep a transformed heart. Your confession of peace and holiness will have you gravitate toward people to increase your own life.

"But you have an anointing from the Holy One, and you know all things." 1 John 2:20 NKJ

"Live creatively, friends. If someone falls into sin, forgivingly restore him, saving your critical comments for yourself. You might be needing forgiveness before the day's out." Galatians 6:1 MB

"Follow peace with all men, and holiness, without which no man shall see the Lord" Hebrews 12:15

Doing great miracles require great faith. If the Spirit wants you to do greater works, and He does, you can search for the glory in you to produce the harvest from his Seed. God has entrusted you with His Spirit. You can develop a relationship with the kind of power that exceeds your limits and depends on His limitless ability. You can follow Him beyond what you know into a place that's reserved for the obedient and faithful, who are rewarded for their diligence.

"...he cares enough to respond to those who seek him."
Hebrews 11:6 MB

The promises of God do not stop with eternal life. Our reality in life is what God says. When we get to the point when we only believe what he says, our dominion becomes drastically evident in this place and time;

"These miraculous signs will accompany those who believe: They will cast out demons in my name, and they will speak in new languages. They will be able to handle snakes with safety, and if they drink anything poisonous, it won't hurt them. They will be able to place their hands on the sick, and they will be healed." Mark 16:17, 18 NLT

Your personal faith in the word is in what you expect God to do. When you read the word it sows the seed. When you pray, it waters the seed. Your growth lies in your consistency. Your spiritual relationship grows with knowing you have innumerable things you can ask for.

"I am the Real Vine and my Father is the Farmer. He cuts off every branch of me that doesn't bear grapes. And every branch that is grape-bearing he prunes back so it will bear even more...But if you make yourselves at home with me and my words are at home in you, you can

be sure that whatever you ask will be listened to and acted upon. This is how my Father shows who he is — when you produce grapes, when you mature as my disciples." John 15:2-8 MB

If you don't believe the truth, you'll get a lie because that's all that's left. Since all heaven and hell is fighting for us, there is no neutral ground. We will be victors or victims. We cannot walk by *sight* and expect the Spirit to lead us. Looking at your sins will get you nowhere, but looking towards Jesus will take you to absolute super-natural victory! When you seek those things which are above, you'll find the rewards of your faith in heavenly places with Him.

"Therefore, since we are surrounded by such a huge crowd of witnesses to the life of faith, let us strip off every weight that slows us down, especially the sin that so easily trips us up. And let us run with endurance the race God has set before us. We do this by keeping our eyes on Jesus, the champion who initiates and perfects our faith..." Hebrews 12:1, 2 NLT

When you seek Him, He rewards your faith with the manifested promises of His Word. When God gives you a promise, He is declaring your future and your faith will apprehend it. You believe what is not yet manifested. You receive exactly what you believe for. Since unbelief can have you live well below your Godly inheritance, you need to learn to put absolute confidence in God. Line up every thought with your born again spirit man, that's always connected with God. In any situation, let Faith take the call and be your answering service.

You need to be taught about where you're going and not where you are. You can let the Spirit guide you into the future, or let your '*old man*' live. When you grow from Faith to Faith you become one with the character and nature of the Word and discern quickly what is not of Him. The old man may try to resurrect himself. And with any attention to it, what has been crucified in your life will attempt to cause you to forget. Deactivation is detrimental to all who are out there depending on you. Follow the faith building vision of God.

"For therein is the righteousness of God revealed from faith to faith: as it is written, The just shall live by faith." Romans 1:17

"We were also given absolutely terrific promises to pass on to you-your tickets to participation in the life of God after you turned your back on a world corrupted by lust" 2 Peter 1:4 MB

"My assumption is that you have paid careful attention to him, been well instructed in the truth precisely as we have it in Jesus. Since, then, we do not have the excuse of ignorance, everything—and I do mean everything—connected with that old way of life has to go. It's rotten through and through. Get rid of it! And then take on an entirely new way of life—a God-fashioned life, a life renewed from the inside and working itself into your conduct as God accurately reproduces his character in you." Ephesians 4:21-24 MB

"For if anyone is a hearer of the word and not a doer, he is like a man observing his natural face in a mirror; for he observes himself, goes away, and immediately forgets what kind of man he was." James 1:23, 24 NKJ

The '*old man*' is useless to you and cannot comprehend where you are going. Don't be satisfied with yesterday's accomplishments, but enjoy the abundance of today's revelation and knowledge. Keep pressing toward the mark and high calling of God. Recognize what makes you weak and resist it. When you let go of everything you have, you receive everything that Jesus has.

"When I was a child, I spake as a child, I understood as a child, I thought as a child: but when I became a man, I put away childish things." 1 Corinthians 13:11

"I'm not saying that I have this all together, that I have it made. But I am well on my way, reaching out for Christ, who has so wondrously reached out for me. Friends, don't get me wrong: By no means do I count myself an expert in all of this, but I've got my eye on the goal, where God is beckoning us onward to Jesus. I'm off and running and I'm not turning back." Philippians 3:13, 14 MB

Faith is part of the reality of God. Faith is the supernatural existence to aid you to live in your God given destiny. Faith puts a demand on the gifts of the Spirit. Faith takes you from I can't; to I can. His Word is your divine right. It is not enough to know that God can do His promises. You have to know them and fight for them because of hindering forces around you. Our anointing will be directly proportional to the time we spend searching after the things of God. You must maintain your confidence. God is looking for people who are impressed with Him. If you could *'take it or leave it'* you are not called to do it.

"For as the body without the spirit is dead, so faith without works is dead also." James 2:26

When God reveals to you who you are in Jesus, and what you can do in prayer, you will get His direction, revelation and transformation. Wherever you go in prayer, with the influence of God's nature, the miracles will follow you. God believes in prayer. After you received the revelation of how powerful your prayer is and you bless Him with the proper prayer that He is waiting for, he will hear you over millions, compared to those without confidence. Then you will get into the dimension that you get whatever you ask. Don't let anyone tell you you're a flop when you have Christ in you.

"And whatever things you ask in prayer, believing, you will receive." Matthew 21:22 NKJ

You can walk in the newness of life, understanding the supernatural provision that He has for you and become bold in your prayer life. When you ask anything from God as a son or daughter, the answer from heaven is no different between you and Jesus. We pray in Faith because when we see the promise in the Word. We contend for this Faith because we have to fight for what we believe in. When we believe the Word, We act on it and will make the most out of the opportunities presented to us and lift the expectations of others. You must pursue your potential in Christ in a much higher level then where you are. Miracles will start happening quickly as you reject Adam's fallen nature. There is no ceiling to God's power. There is no end to His provision.

"...I have to write insisting and begging that you fight with everything you have in you for this faith entrusted to us as a gift to guard and cherish." Jude 1:3 MB

We need to understand the power needed for these days. There is no shortage of power, but knowledge. If we wavier, we lose our sense of power, anointing and authority. And you won't get far if you think you're a sinner or begging to try and get a prayer through. When you continue to walk in the Spirit the power becomes more familiar. One of the deceptions of the enemy is to make you believe that God changes his mind and prayer is like rolling the dice. God never changes, but people will change with the power of God. The time is coming and now is that the difference between the powerful and the powerless are becoming more evident. When we enforce the power that we already have, the Spirit takes a hold of us to get rid of the darkness of the world together with him. A mystery of God is to find out how full of God we really are.

"He will flatter and win over those who have violated the covenant. But the people who know their God will be strong and will resist him." Daniel 11:32 NLT

"Now to him that is of power to stablish you according to my gospel, and the preaching of Jesus Christ, according to the revelation of the mystery, which was kept secret since the world began, But now is made manifest, and by the scriptures of the prophets, according to the commandment of the everlasting God, made known to all nations for the obedience of faith" Romans 16:25, 26

What we receive is what we can perceive by faith. We can believe like Jesus believed. We cannot regard iniquity in our hearts and waver and expect God to answer our prayer nor can we have an evil conscience or a bad perception of our selves. If we have a slight apprehension that something bad might happen again or a family disease history, we are looking back at the world's calendar and putting a big 'target' on our back for the enemy. When we have absolute confidence in God, we possess the God kind of faith.

"If I regard iniquity in my heart, the Lord will not hear me" Psalm 66:18

"But let him ask in faith, with no doubting, for he who doubts is like a wave of the sea driven and tossed by the wind. For let not that man suppose that he will receive anything from the Lord." James 1:6, 7 NKJ

"The worst of my fears has come true, what I've dreaded most has happened." Job 3:25 MB

God granted us full 'dunamis' power *after* He resurrected (Acts 1:8). We are cleansed by the blood of the lamb and declared righteous by His resurrection. We can be confident when we guard our heart from the thief. We must have the realization of the fact that we are clean and be comfortable in His holy place. We are entitled to have the same relationship with God as Jesus did (Philipians 2:5, 6).

"Guard your heart more than any treasure, for it is the source of all life." Proverbs 4:23 NEB

Whatever harvest a person sows, he will reap. If one is satisfied with their current harvest, they are backsliding. Many experiences in churches these days fall short of New Testament experience. You should be willing to step out and raise the bar on your harvest field unless you want to keep what the enemy has given to us. Nobody can expect change, if the only reference is what they've been through. A large percentage of people who listen to the Word don't expect change. Many preachers don't even preach change or repentance.

The quickest way to fall is to say '*I can always repent later*'. If we fall, our reputation and confidence others have in us weaken. The shortage of a holy lifestyle will have many go to night clubs, backslide and create divisions in church or depend on the media for their spiritual education. It also cuts off the longevity needed in a long term relationship.

"...It means we'd better get on with it. Strip down, start running—and never quit! No extra spiritual fat, no parasitic sins. Keep your eyes on Jesus, who both began and finished this race we're in. Study how he did it. Because he never lost sight of where he was headed—that exhilarating finish in and with God—he could put up with anything along the way: Cross, shame, whatever. And now he's there, in the place of honor, right alongside God. When you find yourselves flagging in your faith, go over that story again, item by item, that long litany of hostility he plowed through. That will shoot adrenaline into your souls!" Hebrews 12:1-3 MB**

We cannot live as if there is no plan. Our results in God come in direct proportion to the revelation that we have in a particular area. When you move away from your natural senses and tap into the power of God that resides in you, you will experience God's knowledge, insight and the supernatural.

We need to consistently exercise our Faith to build spiritual muscles. By starting out with easier things like headaches or warts and growing to stronger things, our faith will grow with exercise and patience. Every Spirit involved victory will increase it. Knowledge will strengthen it. We must know where to plug it in. Even King David started out with a lion and a bear before facing Goliath. The people around him began to have confidence in him because of his previous Spirit involved victories.

"I have done this to both lions and bears, and I'll do it to this pagan Philistine, too, for he has defied the armies of the living God! The Lord who rescued me from the claws of the lion and the bear will rescue me from this Philistine!'" 1 Samuel 17:36, 37 NLT

All people start with a measure of Faith. What you do with it determines the victories in your life. Your faith will grab all the promises available through the Word. Your relationship with God will have a daily flow. The flow is always in the now. It is not living in yesterday's bread, or by having *heard* the Word, but active hearing and meditation. Hope will be for the future, but Faith is in the now. There are certain areas we will excel easier than others, but there is a place like worship where we can all flow easily. In some cases, we don't have time to think, but act. Someone who has the Holy Spirit and doesn't know Him is trouble. We must grow into the knowledge of His benefits and live by faith in what the Spirit teaches us.

"For I say, through the grace given to me, to everyone who is among you, not to think *of himself* more highly than he ought to think, but to think soberly, as God has dealt to each one a measure of faith." Romans 12:3 NKJ

"I have more understanding than all my teachers, for Your testimonies are my meditation." Psalm 119:99 NKJ

"Bless the LORD, O my soul; And all that is within me, bless His holy name! Bless the LORD, O my soul, And forget not all His benefits: Who forgives all your iniquities, Who heals all your diseases" Psalm 103:2, 3 NKJ

When Faith is big your love is big. When Faith has its perfect work, it brings patience to overcome oppositions. We can then move up to an 'inside the veil' associate level with God.

"But their minds were blinded. For until this day the same veil remains unlifted in the reading of the Old Testament,

because the *veil* is taken away in Christ." 2 Corinthians 3:14 NKJ

"This *hope* we have as an anchor of the soul, both sure and steadfast, and which enters the *Presence* behind the veil" Hebrews 6:19 NKJ

"But let patience have *its* perfect work, that you may be perfect and complete, lacking nothing." James 1:4 NKJ

Faith is governed by the full Word of God, and is nothing less than expecting His promises. Anytime you have a hunger for God, the Holy Spirit is obligated to feed you through His Word and build you up. This increase eliminates the worries and the '*what ifs*'. Faith is a confident assurance, being sure, positive and certain for that which is hoped for and is not here yet. Faith is a spiritual force that comes when you hear the Word that awakens the message inside you. True understanding is this: knowing the victory is already yours through Christ.

"NOW FAITH is the assurance (the confirmation, the title deed) of the things [we] hope for, being the proof of things [we] do not see and the conviction of their reality [faith perceiving as real fact what is not revealed to the senses]." Hebrews 11:1 AMP

"Faith is the confidence that what we hope for will actually happen; it gives us assurance about things we cannot see" Hebrews 11:1 NLT

"The fundamental fact of existence is that this trust in God, this faith, is the firm foundation under everything that makes life worth living. It's our handle on what we can't see." Hebrews 11:1 MB

We can let God be our attorney in the court of life and let Him speak instead of us. He is the link between our born again spirit and all the untapped, limitless supernatural resources that are available in the spirit realm. From our heart within us will flow rivers of living water. He is not slack. We can believe and proclaim the Word followed by the demonstration of the Spirit's power.

"He who believes in Me, as the Scripture has said, out of his heart will flow rivers of living water." John 7:38 NKJ

"The Lord is not slack concerning his promise..." 2 Peter 3:9

The same grace that saves you changes you and resurrects your life. You have an audience with God. Where God lives, His power is present to heal, deliver and set free. Christianity is an experience, not a mindset. Promotion comes because you know what God has promised and you believe it. You have the potential to be all or nothing with God. Let the Word elevate you so that God can be seen from within you. The anointing you have today is more powerful than the opposition. Your faith will make you whole.

"Now ye are clean through the word which I have spoken unto you." John 15:3

"...Arise, go your way. Your faith has made you well." Luke 17:19 NKJ

CHAPTER 12

Miracles

God didn't make a mistake when He called you. Through all of us, Jesus is doing more now than He ever did. You will always have supernatural help. Even if you get off track, the anointing is present to lead you back to your destiny.

The ability to do miracles depends on your ability to unleash the power of resident faith in you. When you get confidence, you should never throw it away by entertaining another opinion. When you have the confidence of the outcome, you can speak the outcome to temporary circumstances. When your compassion overrides sympathy you will be accompanied with the belief that you can do something about unfavorable circumstances. It takes active faith to do God's work. You can't operate by religion or our old teacher of works, which was performance orientated, but faith only. Faith and religion never mix.

"So do not throw away this confident trust in the Lord. Remember the great reward it brings you!" Hebrews 10:35 NLT

"Wherefore the law was our schoolmaster to bring us unto Christ, that we might be justified by faith. But after that faith is come, we are no longer under a schoolmaster." Galatians 3:24, 25

"But now we are delivered from the law, that being dead wherein we were held; that we should serve in newness of spirit, and not in the oldness of the letter." Romans 7:6

Once you receive the revelation of what Christ did for you, and who you are in Him, you are able to pull the trigger on the inside which releases power to do miracles. Miracles will become so simple that you would have a hard time not expecting them to happen. They must be anticipated and invited. By answering the call to operate in this realm, you will heal the sick, raise the dead and cast out devils.

"Heal the sick, cleanse the lepers, raise the dead, cast out devils..." Matthew 10:8

"Also I heard the voice of the Lord, saying, Whom shall I send, and who will go for us? Then said I, Here am I; send me." Isaiah 6:8

Miracles don't just happen. The gift of God has to be stirred up in us, not figured out. When you stir up the gift within you, you tap into the resident power and angelic help of God, divine relationships and friendships. When you have a revelation of how much God loves you, your faith improves. When you see the value He has put on you, it increases your belief in His nature of love and His blood covenant for us. When you turn on love and compassion when you speak to people, these Words will heal and fulfill. The anointing helps you see and helps you say. The Spirit will guide us when we are willing and win daily battles with our flesh.

"For this reason I remind you to fan into flame the gift of God..." 2 Timothy 1:6 NKJ

"...Yes, I have loved you with an everlasting love; Therefore with lovingkindness I have drawn you." Jeremiah 31:3 NKJ

"...the spirit indeed is willing, but the flesh is weak." Matthew 26:41

"...lead the life of the Spirit; then you will never satisfy the passions of the flesh." Galatians 5:16 Mof

To be a minister of performance, you must have an expectancy of transformation. You must have a direct deposit of the word for divine revelation, utterance and ability to walk in power and demonstrations. The things He reveals are pertinent to change your life and reveal God through you. God gives you revelation so that you can do something with it.

"And the second came, saying, 'Master, your mina has earned five minas.' Likewise he said to him, 'You also be over five cities.'" Luke 19:18, 19 NKJ

The manifestations will come in your life when you need them for yourself or someone else. Meditate on the Word of God until the manifestation comes to the authority you already have. If there is no proof of the Holy Spirit in our lives, no one can benefit. If we teach that only 'special' people can give the manifestations, we are not glorifying God. We are not here to make dependents, but disciples. They should be ready for a spiritual transaction and transformation of their lives. Faith is simply using what belongs to all of us. We are here to make a contribution to eternity. Continue to believe that God gave you what you asked for when you prayed, thanking and praising Him for what He has given, and it will always materialize.

"Don't worry about anything; instead, pray about everything. Tell God what you need, and thank him for all he has done." Philippians 4:6 NLT

When we come out of our *'put up with'* or *'settle for'* mindset, unto the 'done deal' there won't be a burden for us to carry. The anointing will make your victory a reality, no matter what the circumstances. The anointing will take you into the realm of 'always yes' promises of God. God backs up faith, not effort. God made faith so that we could cooperate with His help without human effort. When what you believe is beyond your ability to manipulate, you step into a higher realm of faith. When you are totally dependent on God, the dynamics of the Spirit will manifest.

"Then Jesus said, "Come to me, all of you who are weary and carry heavy burdens, and I will give you rest." Matthew 11:28 NLT

"Casting all your care upon him; for he cares for you." 1 Peter 5:7 NKJ

"And it shall come to pass in that day, that his burden shall be taken away...and the yoke shall be destroyed because of the anointing." Isaiah 10:27

"Whatever God has promised gets stamped with the Yes of Jesus. In him, this is what we preach and pray, the great Amen, God's Yes and our Yes together, gloriously evident." 2 Corinthians 1:20 MB

"...Not by might, nor by power, but by my spirit, saith the LORD of hosts." Zechariah 4:6

We don't have to wish for a miracle, but connect people with the Word to receive what all people are searching for. God is not moved by the needs of suffering people, but you are here to move on His behalf with the power He has given you with His faith giving words. If nobody else is doing it around you, don't let that stop you from being a pioneer. Let the truth be known. God reveals truth, so you will have a guide for life. The highest thing He can give you is His Word.

"True, some of them were unfaithful; but just because they were unfaithful, does that mean God will be unfaithful? Of course not! Even if everyone else is a liar, God is true." Romans 3:3, 4 NLT

"...for You have magnified Your word above all Your name." Psalm 138:2 NKJ

The supernatural realm of God is here for us to change the natural realm. It requires boldness in the spirit. In the land of the living, we are in the decision making realm. If you waited for God to move on somebody, or prayed at home hoping someone else would intervene, you would only see a few miracles in your lifetime. It is God's will for you to perform miracles by replenishing the earth with God.

You are a champion. You are endued; or clothed with power to become proof providers of the resurrection of Jesus and activity of the Holy Spirit. You are clothed with what goes beyond your natural nature. You will revolutionize the territory of your known jurisdiction. You wear the antidote of what goes beyond imaginations. People will feel comfortable around you because you're wearing a miracle. You know when you hear from God, that it's a done deal. You don't have to be afraid to promise it, because God will always back it up. Your inspired utterance is filled with the potential for the miraculous, waiting for receivership of expectation at the other end. Because the character of God is to give you abundantly more than you can ask or think, you should never underestimate the power of your utterance.

When you show up, God shows up. When the angels tell you of an assignment and are ready to carry it out and eject spirits of pain, or spirits of infirmities, the word of knowledge will come to you so they can move on the voice of God. The demons see the invisible forces and know they are being served an eviction notice, and have to leave. Before you speak, whether at a bus stop, or a large crowd, they will look in advance for places to run and hide. You listen to His utterance, and then transform that miracle working power out of your mouth to perform what He said He would do. He thinks it, we listen and then we speak it. No Word of God is devoid of power.

"And now I will send the Holy Spirit, just as my Father promised. But stay here in the city until the Holy Spirit comes and fills you with power from heaven." Luke 24:49 NLT

"Now unto him that is able to do exceeding abundantly above all that we ask or think, according to the power that worketh in us" Ephesians 3:20

"So shall My word be that goes forth from My mouth; It shall not return to Me void, But it shall accomplish what I please, And it shall prosper *in the thing* for which I sent it." Isaiah 55:11 NKJ

You are a working thermostat, not a thermometer. Your enlightment and enthusiasm will elevate other miracle workers. Your obstacle eliminating knowledge will fill your atmosphere wherever your feet walk with faith. You won't have to wait for *'the water to be stirred'* when you know there's a river coming out of you. You learn to cut the enemy off at the first sign, first sniffle, and first symptom so that the toe-hold doesn't become a stronghold. You know the Spirit of the Lord is upon you to give liberty, freedom and deliverance. You know there's the ability to lay hands on people without a word. You know there's the potential to go boldly where no man has gone before.

"God's Spirit is on me; he's chosen me to preach the Message of good news to the poor, Sent me to announce pardon to prisoners and recovery of sight to the blind, To set the burdened and battered free, to announce, "This is God's year to act!""" Luke 4:18 MB

"And when Jesus was come into Peter's house, he saw his wife's mother laid, and sick of a fever. And he touched her hand, and the fever left her..." Matthew 8:14, 15

"And there are also many other things which Jesus did, the which, if they should be written every one, I suppose that even the world itself could not contain the books that should be written. Amen." John 21:25

"Verily, verily, I say unto you, He that believeth on me, the works that I do shall he do also; and greater works than these shall he do; because I go unto my Father. And whatsoever ye shall ask in my name, that will I do..." John 14:12, 13

CHAPTER 13

Intercession for God's people: Preparing Yourself

Our personal intercession guided by the Holy Spirit will be world changing according to prophecy. We can take every opportunity to pray and intercede for anyone we see without contacting them, boosting each in prayer and hope of salvation. It also keeps our own mind spiritual in unifying our thought life with the participation of God in our pathways.

"And he gave some, apostles; and some, prophets; and some, evangelists; and some, pastors and teachers; For the perfecting of the saints, for the work of the ministry, for the edifying of the body of Christ: Till we all come in the unity of the faith, and of the knowledge of the Son of God, unto a perfect man, unto the measure of the stature of the fulness of Christ" Ephesians 4:11-13

"Moreover as for me, God forbid that I should sin against the LORD in ceasing to pray for you..." 1 Samuel 12:23

"I exhort therefore, that, first of all, supplications, prayers, intercessions, and giving of thanks, be made for all men" 1 Timothy 2:1

We are saved to save others and healed to heal others. The New Testament's Greek word *sozo* is used interchangeably for being saved or healed. When our mind is renewed to accept the power we have through simple faith, we grow in faith to do greater works. Whether you're a mother with children or a modern day apostle, you can take advantage of knowing your God given spiritual benefits and experience the manifestations of God and help the body of Christ become more confident in the area of prayer ministry.

If you want more people to have healing and miracles, pray for more people. Even If you prayed for ten deaf people and only one gets healed, you're doing better than one who never tries. God wants you to change your agenda to His. Have a desire to see healings for the glory of God (*and not yourself*), and your faith will unlock the door to these gifts.

"And stop assuming an outward expression that does not come from within you and is not representative of what you are in your inner being but is patterned after this age; but change your outward expression to one that comes within and is representative of your inner being, by the renewing of your mind, resulting in your putting to the test what is the will of God, the good and well-pleasing and complete will, and having found that it meets specifications, place your approval on it." Romans 12:2 KW

"...the righteousness of God revealed from faith to faith: as it is written, The just shall live by faith." Romans 1:17

"Ask, and it will be given to you; seek, and you will find; knock, and it will be opened to you. For everyone who

asks receives, and he who seeks finds, and to him who knocks it will be opened." Matthew 7:7, 8 NKJ

"So you should earnestly desire the most helpful gifts." 1 Corinthians 12:31 NLT

If you fellowship at a place that doesn't know and teach your authority, they are likely to bury you early (*or you them*). A person who talks about what God doesn't do, instead of what He does, is putting his focus on the world system of failure. The preached word of uncertainty, wavering or unbelief is not a good diet. We have been so far behind since the days of the book of Acts, that we need more seeds planted in us to turn our meditation over to the truth.

"I know that as soon as I'm gone, vicious wolves are going to show up and rip into this flock, men from your very own ranks twisting words so as to seduce disciples into following them instead of Jesus. So stay awake and keep up your guard…Now I'm turning you over to God, our marvelous God whose gracious Word can make you into what he wants you to be and give you everything you could possibly need in this community of holy friends." Acts 20:29-32 MB

"People will be lovers of themselves…having a form of godliness but denying its power. Have nothing to do with them." 2 Timothy 3:2-5 NKJ

The truth will only make you free if you know it. Grace was preached by Martin Luther in the 16th century and still, many people don't have enough seed planted and feel they need works to add to the atonement of Christ. Healing has been increasingly preached in the last 50 years and we have seen more people lay hold unto this truth then we have in the last 1000. It is not that the miracles have stopped in the 1ˢᵗ century (*like some people may say based on experience or alternate interpretation*), but God's ways are the same and don't change just because many have stopped preaching it. In the last ten years we have seen more miracles in the last 50 and we are getting to the same point where everyone is healed in a Holy Spirit led service. We are free, when we know what to do with the truth we know.

"Whatever is good and perfect comes down to us from God our Father, who created all the lights in the heavens. He never changes or casts a shifting shadow." James 1:17 NLT

"...and how shall they believe in him of whom they have not heard? and how shall they hear without a preacher? And how shall they preach, except they be sent? as it is written, How beautiful are the feet of them that preach the gospel of peace, and bring glad tidings of good things!" Romans 10:14, 15

"And you shall know the truth, and the truth shall make you free." John 8:32 NKJ

We are decision makers (*not the angels*). We live by the fruit of our mouth. Many people in and outside the church are looking to us for examples. There is such an unlimited potential in Christ, we need to constantly feed on His Word to run our own race of destiny with so many lifeless words from the opposition.

Jesus loves our faith. He is praying that it never fails. It is our mutual faith that brings promises to life. Our faith begins when we recognize Him as Lord. In time we develop an intimacy with Him and learn of His easy yoke of freedom.

We can help others better when we have full confidence in what He's done for us personally.

"But I have prayed for you, that your faith should not fail..." Luke 22:32 NKJ

"For I long to see you, that I may impart unto you some spiritual gift, to the end ye may be established; That is, that I may be comforted together with you by the mutual faith both of you and me." Romans 1:12, 13

The trial of our faith is precious to Him as we rise above obstacles in trusting His Word above all we see in the natural. In our trials, there is a Judge, jury, prosecutor and Defendant. The accusing enemy will immediately attempt to steal your seed by breathing an opinion at you that's different from God, to make you weigh circumstantial evidence over fact. If you have a track record of changing your mind, the enemy will try to talk you out of what you have so don't let the seed fall down by the wayside. Right now, God wants to put some 'Miracle grow' on it. You do your part by putting down every imagination that is against God's will. He does His part by blessing (or empowering to prosper) all that is within your soul. Let every part of your body be touched by the Presence of God. Pray into the yes and amen of God and be confident with the answer before it happens. Come into His unseen alter and get freedom from your yesterday. Get to know that place of peace that not only happened when you got saved, but is available continuously to the point where people can perceive it upon you. People will see you living in His word by your obstacle denouncing faith.

"That the genuineness of your faith, *being* much more precious than gold that perishes, though it is tested by

fire, may be found to praise, honor, and glory at the reve-lation of Jesus Christ" 1 Peter 1:7 MB

"A double minded man is unstable in all his ways." James 1:8

"casting down arguments and every high thing that exalts itself against the knowledge of God, bringing every thought into captivity to the obedience of Christ, and being ready to punish all disobedience when your obedi-ence is fulfilled." 2 Corinthians 10:5, 6 NKJ

"You will keep *him* in perfect peace, *Whose* mind *is* stayed *on You,* Because he trusts in You." Isaiah 26:3 NKJ

In the areas we are not strong in, we should keep appro-priate verses around our 'eye gates' in our homes, walls, wallets or purses to have a spiritual medicine around. Your prayer time should include assurance, boldness and confi-dence in with the peace of God. Your praying in tongues will also build yourself up. When you pray that you may interpret your tongues, your confidence will increase as God is revealing the mysteries you are saying when you speak to Him. You should pray for opportunities of divine appoint-ments to exercise your faith. Singing, praise and worship music is a big benefit to uplift yourself or others that you minister to for spiritual medicine.

"So anyone who speaks in tongues should pray also for the ability to interpret what has been said." 1 Corinthians 14:13 NLT

"For if you have the ability to speak in tongues, you will be talking only to God, since people won't be able to understand you. You will be speaking by the power of the

Spirit, but it will all be mysterious." 1 Corinthians 14:2 NLT

"A person who speaks in tongues is strengthened personally..." 1 Corinthians 14:4 NLT

"...Well then, what shall I do? I will pray in the spirit, and I will also pray in words I understand. I will sing in the spirit, and I will also sing in words I understand." 1 Corinthians 14:15 NLT

"So, when you pray in your private prayer language, don't hoard the experience for yourself. Pray for the insight and ability to bring others into that intimacy." 1 Corinthians 14:13 MB

"...David took an harp, and played with his hand: so Saul was refreshed, and was well, and the evil spirit departed from him." 1 Samuel 16:23

When you know the ability is not coming from you, it relieves you of the awareness of physical weakness and limitations. Your point of contact is higher than yourself. Smith Wigglesworth who had many miracles in his life including raising 26 people from the dead, continued to perform miracles during a battle with kidney stones. Peter Pretorius who performs creative miracles in these days began healing people with the power of God while he was still smoking (although he quit shortly after). God is not trying to make you a magician to promote you, but does things for his glory and his people. He only has fallible vessels to work with. And we all have spiritual growing to do. We don't have to preach about us if we preach Jesus.

"God's gifts and God's call are under full warranty— never canceled, never rescinded." Romans 11:29 MB

"Preach the word; be prepared in season, out of season…" 2 Timothy 4:2 NKJ

Part of building the belief system in God in your environment requires to plant seeds of unity in love, including not talking bad about another member of the body of Christ (*different denominations, preachers, leaders, church members, etc.*) Even if people have different methods than you favor, their good intentions and harvest will manifest over time. Plant good seed on your own harvest that you've been given. Find the good or God in people and continue in optimism in God's promise. God will sort it out in judgment day. Unity and intimacy with God is always more important than the miracles. This will also apply when you pray for people without judging. When we see saved people who are recipients of our prayers, we must see them justified as God does; who has no respect of persons.

"John said to Jesus, 'Master, we saw someone using your name to cast out demons, but we told him to stop because he isn't in our group.' But Jesus said, 'Don't stop him! Anyone who is not against you is for you.' " Luke 9:49, 50 NLT

"My dear brothers and sisters, how can you claim to have faith in our glorious Lord Jesus Christ if you favor some people over others?...doesn't this discrimination show that your judgments are guided by evil motives?" James 2:1, 4 NLT

"But the voice spoke again: "Do not call something unclean if God has made it clean." Acts 10:15 NLT

"The farmer's workers went to him and said, 'Sir, the field where you planted that good seed is full of weeds! Where did they come from?' 'An enemy has done this!' the farmer exclaimed. 'Should we pull out the weeds?' they asked. 'No,' he replied, 'you'll uproot the wheat if you do. Let both grow together until the harvest. Then I will tell the harvesters to sort out the weeds, tie them into bundles, and burn them, and to put the wheat in the barn." Matthew 13:27-30 NLT

What comes out of our mouths shapes our lives and the lives of others. Jesus never taught that disease was always the fault of a sinner. He would always rather choose mercy than wrath for His people. His disciples bought into this doctrine because they have been taught it and have not made the transition into the discovery of His grace;

"As Jesus was walking along, he saw a man who had been blind from birth. 'Rabbi,' his disciples asked him, 'why was this man born blind? Was it because of his own sins or his parents' sins?' 'It was not because of his sins or his parents' sins,' Jesus answered. 'This happened so the power of God could be seen in him.' " John 9:1-3 NLT

"He does not punish us for all our sins; he does not deal harshly with us, as we deserve. For his unfailing love toward those who fear him is as great as the height of the heavens above the earth." Psalm 103:10, 11 NLT

Your view in the unseen has to be a lot more substance than the '*seen*' world. You have more power than you need but you have to have the knowledge of how to tap into it. You can have a light switch, but never turn it on and find yourself sitting in the dark. It's the diligent seekers of God that will be rewarded. The mediocre Christians will never think about using the power they have if they never pursue it or know it's available. When more Christians get a hold of the vision and use their faith, it's *really* going to be over for the devil. Until then, many will perish. We need to experience the God kind of faith: The faith that He gave to us.

"When people do not accept divine guidance, they run wild. But whoever obeys the law is joyful." Proverbs 29:18 NLT

"My people are ruined because they don't know what's right or true..." Hosea 4:6 MB

Preparing Others

You need to know your identity, your righteousness or right standing with God, and justification, so people will know you are sent. If not, you will not be able to pray super-naturally for them. When you live a Word filled lifestyle, you are convincing when you speak. The truth in your life comes out of sub-conscious into your voice. When you have an 'inside the veil' experience, people will notice your anointing. A blind man will know beyond the shadow of a doubt, that you have the anointing to heal him. Your words will be wings instead of chains. You will not have a liberal society way of thinking but a liberating one. People will see in your eyes that you know, that you know, that you know. They also need to expect that you are able to bring them healing. Look how Jesus interviews the blind man;

"And when he was come into the house, the blind men came to him: and Jesus saith unto them, <u>Believe ye that I am able to do this?</u> They said unto him, Yea, Lord. Then touched he their eyes, saying, According to your faith be it unto you." Matthew 9:28, 29

Some will Place a demand on the anointing, but others need more Word. Let people know they can trust in His Yes, and get excited. Give an injection from the Spirit to replace the input from the world. Tell them that His name is I AM, not *I was*. Let people know that all His names are effective. Let people know they can trust in His Yes, and anticipate a miracle.

"Then Moses said to God, 'Indeed, *when* I come to the children of Israel and say to them, 'The God of your fathers has sent me to you,' and they say to me, 'What *is* His name?' what shall I say to them?' And God said to Moses, 'I AM WHO I AM...'" Exodus 3:13, 14 NKJ

There are cases where roots run very deep with faith in dire situations. It may take a 'ton' of word to make up for an ounce of bad understanding. For example; it would be easier to teach prosperity in America than in poor parts of India or Africa. However, if you had a miracle to jump start faith in their atmosphere, the belief system would increase quickly. One of my associate ministers was in Vietnam and after she prayed and a man rose up from the dead, people changed their old religions and accepted miracle power. Dennis Balcombe who leads in missionary work in China tells of one province, after witnessing two people raised up from the dead, went from 3,000 Christians to 3,000,000 within two years. Great miracles can uproot dire straits.

"Unless you *people* see signs and wonders, you will by no means believe." John 4:48 NKJ

"And the people with one accord gave heed unto those things which Philip spake, hearing and seeing the miracles which he did." Acts 8:6

It can help to be around other people who have a ministry of healing, deliverance or miracles and be in prayer with them. You can hang out with champions like Stephan did (Acts 6) or Elisha (2 Kings 3) who poured water on the hands of Elijah before God sends you out. Make sure you are a person who is sent; *not just went.* You should be around someone who encourages and teaches you and also have peers on your level as well as opportunities to share the gospel and teach others how to touch people with God. Don't hang around *'bench warmers'* when God has called you to greatness.

You don't have to fight the devil, but your fight is against his methods. This is not the human effort of religion but His indwelling. We use our Holy Ghost backed words to establish our victory. We are not in a war, but a takeover. We speak to situations and not about them. Our goal should be to make the blood, the word and the name of Jesus famous by equipping more laborers for the harvest. He left us in charge. If your flesh or even the devil tells you different; tell him he has the wrong guy!

"Put on the whole armor of God, that you may be able to stand against the wiles of the devil. For we do not wrestle against flesh and blood, but against principalities, against powers, against the rulers of the darkness of this age, against spiritual *hosts* of wickedness in the heavenly *places*." Ephesians 6:11, 12 NKJ

"Then He said to them, "The harvest truly *is* great, but the laborers *are* few; therefore pray the Lord of the harvest to send out laborers into His harvest." Luke 10:2 NKJ

Even with Jesus there were challenges and potential for failure. There were crowds that were not ready, but needed to get ready. There were crowds who judged because of familiarity. Some people may judge us if they knew our past or if we get too personal with people. We need to be sensitive to who our crowd is and where they are at spiritually. The Holy Spirit will show you who will receive and who won't.

"Then Jesus told them, "A prophet is honored everywhere except in his own hometown and among his own family." And so he did only a few miracles there because of their unbelief." Matthew 13:56, 57 NLT

"There was a man in Lystra who couldn't walk. He sat there, crippled since the day of his birth. He heard Paul talking, and Paul, looking him in the eye, saw that he was ripe for God's work, ready to believe. So he said, loud enough for everyone to hear, "Up on your feet!" The man was up in a flash-jumped up and walked around as if he'd been walking all his life." Acts 14:8, 9 MB

We cannot just go to a hospital and clear it out (unless directly inspired by God), we follow and lead others with the Spirit of God. When you paint the same picture in your mind into someone else's; it's called 'practical impartation'. People may be so far away of knowing God's nature, that they feel like Adam did when God wanted to make him a coat but he hid himself in the garden (Gen 3). Sometimes it's not so much the devil telling them they're guilty, but when someone spends a lot of time listening to words from the opposition, they have a tendency to adapt to the feelings of guilt and condemnation the enemy lives in.

When speaking to a person, they cannot be healed beyond their knowledge. There must be something said or done for them to change their belief system. It has to have power that exceeds anything man can generate. Look into their eyes and let them see your confidence. Look for the potential of a needy person and feed their faith with what they need.

And Peter, fastening his eyes upon him with John, said, Look on us... " Acts 3:4

One man wasn't sure if it was the will of Jesus for him to be healed;

"And behold, a leper came and worshiped Him, saying, "Lord, <u>if You are willing</u>, You can make me clean." Then **Jesus put out *His* hand and touched him, saying, "<u>I am willing</u>; be cleansed." Immediately his leprosy was cleansed." Matthew 8:2, 3 NKJ**

If you see someone who is unsure, you can ask them what they expect. Another reason to do this is because if you have another next person in line, you may decrease their expectations because of another person's unbelief. Someone with '*I hope so*' faith is not as inspiring to others as 'Just say the word' faith. The moment people start thinking about what is not happening, the anointing will wane because of the opportunity the enemy has to give his opinion to people who are ready to receive. Keep control with the situation with your confident words.

There are times when people will receive a steady stream of healing over time according to their faith. Compared to a miracle this develops precious faith with a relationship in the Lord is over time instead of a one-time event. God will guide our hearts and reveal to us His pathways because we've chosen to serve Him and His people.

"And let the peace (soul harmony which comes) from Christ rule (act as umpire continually) in your hearts [deciding and settling with finality all questions that arise in your minds, in that peaceful state] to which as [members of Christ's] one body you were also called [to

live]. And be thankful (appreciative), [giving praise to God always]." Colossians 3:15 AMP

"The fact is, God, the Master, does nothing without first telling his prophets the whole story." Amos 3:7 MB

Our faith in the Word is what we expect God to do. Faith should be in the correct tense (i.e. all *have* sinned, not continue to sin). The bible says by His stripes you **were** healed. The faith connection is in the now God, not the hope for the God of the future. If this was so, you would just wait for it in the eternity of heaven.

"...by whose stripes you <u>were</u> healed." 1 Peter 2:24 NKJ

It pleases God for you to believe in Him and you are rewarded when your faith is strong. You are anointed when you teach and preach the kind of faith that people can connect to God with. By the time Jesus tells people to receive according to their faith, seeds are already developed within them. The way you speak with your words can be accepted in the confident manner they are put out with. Your daily confessions to yourself and others materialize into your area of spiritual jurisdiction.

Even though God's nature is a now nature, the body of Christ is catching up to the readiness of His mercy. It helps people to believe God can make a healing manifest immediately, within the hour or over a period of time. Always be ready to be a blessing to someone. Even when you say God bless you, it carries weight. As an apostle, minister or layperson, people are depending on you not to let words your fall to the ground.

"Words kill, words give life; they're either poison or fruit—you choose." Proverbs 18:21 MB

"And Samuel grew, and the LORD was with him, and did let none of his words fall to the ground." 1 Samuel 3:19

If you are not dominating the devil, it is because the devil is dominating you *or* subtly holding you back from being all you can be in the army of God. If you don't have a healthy understanding of your authority, you will be ripped off of the benefits of your life. We do not belong to the god of this world, or the world system. We have been translated out of that system and have *already* over came the enemy. We can't think him out, but we need to speak him out. Even the weakest member of the body has more authority than he does and can say 'you may not devour me in the name of Jesus'. The devil is afraid of authority and does not like embarrassment.

"No one serving as a soldier gets involved in civilian affairs—he wants to please his commanding officer." 2 Timothy 2:4 NKJ

"Blessed *be* the Lord, *Who* daily loads us *with benefits...*" Psalm 68:19 NKJ

"They preached with joyful urgency that life can be radically different; right and left they sent the demons packing; they brought wellness to the sick..." Mark 6:13 MB

If possible, you should not pray alone for deliverance of the opposite sex, or place your hand inappropriately on them. Work as a team when you can. When ministering in deliverance, keep your eyes open and watch out for their deliverance and also for hindrances.

The spirit of doubt is a delaying spirit. He's like a good actor. When you tell him to go, he may have the straightest, most convincing, '*Oscar award winning*' face. But when you resist him, he'll flee from you. When you have a Word on the situation, when you know that the power of Christ in you is stronger than the opposition, you know that defeated spirit is a temporary spirit, waiting to obtain the revelation from you that you know who you are and who God is in you.

"Whereof I am made a minister, according to the dispensation of God which is given to me for you, to fulfil the word of God Even...the riches of the glory of this mystery among the Gentiles; which is Christ in you, the hope of glory" Colossians 1:25-27

"Ye are of God, little children, and have overcome them: because greater is he that is in you, than he that is in the world." 1 John 4:4

In deliverance or praying for someone to be delivered in the presence of God, you should take note to see if someone is either possessed or if they are a true Christian are dealing with oppression, obsession, depression, suppression, repression or just regression. A spirit may need to be cast out first before any healing is done. If they are not a Christian, pray that they receive Jesus as their Savior. Each circumstance will need for the person to modify their lifestyle and get involved with more spiritual activity in their life. One oppressed woman I prayed with actually had demons physically grab her legs and continually haunt her at night so she couldn't get good sleep. After about 20 minutes of praying, she was delivered and slept peacefully from then on. Another lady I met who was suppressed, confused, in pain and out of ministry for years just needed five minutes of reminding her of who she is and always will be in God's eyes to reverse what the enemy had put on her.

When a person is delivered and washed with the water of the word, they have a choice of going back into the world and getting dirty. When Jesus preached the beatitudes, everybody there was already healed before He preached (Matthew 4:24-5:2). In another sermon that required repentance and faith, even many of his disciples turned back. I've even heard of one case where someone was raised from the dead and still went on to lead quite a sinful life. You won't want the same person getting back into you 'prayer line' again or having a condition that has grown worse.

"From that time many of his disciples went back, and walked no more with him." John 6:66

Out of perhaps 30,000 words people hear every day, many people spend a higher percentage of their time watching fictional TV, listening to secular music and hanging out with spiritually weak people. A lot of Christian's burdens are from other Christians. Many people who are interviewed during or after deliverance can testify to the time and place where the symptoms started. Consult with the person you are praying for to see if their practices produce spiritual bondages like fears, addictions, drugs, abuse of authority, corruption, suicidal thoughts, unforgiveness, jealousy, fornication, adultery, tarot card reading, divination or new age movement association among other things designed to take time away from our Creator.

"When an evil spirit leaves a person, it goes into the desert, searching for rest. But when it finds none, it says, 'I will return to the person I came from.' So it returns and finds that its former home is all swept and in order. Then the spirit finds seven other spirits more evil than itself, and they all enter the person and live there. And so that person is worse off than before." Luke 11:24-26 NLT

"For example, never sacrifice your son or daughter as a burnt offering. And do not let your people practice fortune-telling, or use sorcery, or interpret omens, or engage in witchcraft, or cast spells, or function as mediums or psychics, or call forth the spirits of the dead. Anyone who does these things is detestable to the Lord…"
Deuteronomy 18:10-12 NLT

A person who has been directly involved with the occult or witchcraft for years is more likely to take more of your time than someone who has played with a Ouija board or listened to demon inspired music. When I lived in Colorado Springs Colorado, there were many satanic assemblies who would send their children to powerless churches in an attempt to prove their church had more power. It took years of prayer and strategy with city ministry leaders coming together in unity to run them off and make it a leading Christian city that it is today. In order to improve your surroundings, you may need to continue in prayer or sometimes begin a fast, but don't give up. Your fasting should be as the Spirit leads and you may not want to be fasting when you plan to have a big service so that you won't feel weak. When you pray in faith the results are already starting. Many people will continue to be delivered after the prayer since the spirits' holds have been weakened. People who have been deeply affected with the enemy may require more help;

"After arriving back home, his disciples cornered Jesus and asked, "Why couldn't we throw the demon out?" He answered, "There is no way to get rid of this kind of demon except by prayer."" **Mark 9:28, 29 MB**

When this boy was delivered keep in mind that the father was there. If a parent does not approve of the ministry, don't expect the children to stay delivered if they go back to an ungodly house.

Lester Summeral tells the story of a young old boy in the Philippines who was instantly healed of deafness and dumbness in a meeting. He seen him six weeks later with the same problem and his neighbor brought him back. But the boy's parents hated Lester and what he was doing and told him that he had a devil in him to make him speak. They wouldn't feed him. They laughed at him and mimicked him. (*If the head of the house wants the devil there, or is involved with satanic behavior you can't keep him out*) He told the neighbor he would not pray for him unless his own parents brought him.

Notice how Jesus interviews the man for us and the disciples to differentiate that this required more power and steadfast faith;

"He asked the boy's father, "How long has this been going on?" "Ever since he was a little boy. Many times it pitches him into fire or the river to do away with him. If you can do anything, do it. Have a heart and help us!" Jesus said, "If? There are no 'ifs' among believers. Anything can happen.""" Mark 9:21-23 MB

If a person becomes violent, stop praying, or command the spirits to stop showing off (the same way you would if someone is being disruptive during a church service). Pay attention to what God is commanding you to say. If you feel led to place your hand on the affected body parts associated with the spirit, do it. If spirits give body pain, or tighten the person's mouth or throat not to come out, tell them to stop. If they violently shake or fall out under the power of the Spirit wait upon the Lord for direction. Spirits leave easier when your praise God or quote applicable scriptures. All believers will have a tendency to specialize in different areas of ministry, but the more you exercise deliverance the quicker the enemy will recognize your authority.

"...He rebuked the unclean spirit, saying to it, 'Deaf and dumb spirit, I command you, come out of him and enter him no more!' Then *the spirit* cried out, convulsed him greatly, and came out of him. And he became as one dead, so that many said, 'He is dead.' But Jesus took him by the hand and lifted him up, and he arose." Mark 9:25-27 NKJ

"And the evil spirit answered and said, 'Jesus I know, and Paul I know; but who are you?'" Acts 19:15 NKJ

When you feel the heart of God and look for opportunities to bring others into the blessing of the kingdom, He will guide you to them. You'll preach what generates faith. Then, instead of giving alms to the beggar, it will be easier to heal them. You're faith will have no respect of opinions, time or circumstances. People are waiting on someone with the anointing that displays the power of God. You are the person who hears someone needs healing and says; "Let's take care of this right now!" and speak to that situation, whether in a service, your neighborhood, your workplace or any where your feet are with faith.

One day I had a guy come over and work on my house confessing he had a knee problem and thought he needed surgery. I reminded him of what his God does and I quoted Psalm 103 to him. He was immediately healed and went to work on my house without pain.

One time before a service even started a brother told me he had strep throat. Without a word I placed my hand on his neck and he was instantly healed.

"O my soul, bless God, don't forget a single blessing! He forgives your sins—every one. He heals your diseases—every one." **Psalm 103:2, 3 MB**

"And my speech and my preaching was not with enticing words of man's wisdom, but in demonstration of the Spirit and of power. That your faith should not stand in the wisdom of men, but in the power of God." **1 Corinthians 2:4, 5**

Whether you preach, street witness, or share with someone, you need to put it where they can get it. You will also learn to see how much they can receive. Make sure they are in agreement, lest someone is left in disappointment. Give ministry only when a person is ready. Do not let them get in a funk where they think it's just not for them.

Some handicapped people are used to people taking care of themselves may be afraid having responsibility on their own. If some are not healed the first time, the spirit may become more stubborn. Use encouraging words and give scriptures instead of making any excuses. If they have excuses, tell them God's word on the situation as it applies to them.

"When Jesus saw him lying there, and knew that he already had been *in that condition* a long time, He said to him, 'Do you want to be made well?' " **John 5:6 NKJ**

A lady I ministered to told me that's what happens when you get old and that's why her joints were weak with arthritis. When I told her about Caleb being 85 and well, she accepted the condition that God wanted her strong and became stronger right there on the spot. If your expectation is the same, you will have a good connection with God and the Spirit will rush to the power of agreement in prayer.

"...and now, here I am this day, eighty-five years old. As yet I *am as* strong this day as on the day that Moses sent me..." Joshua 14:11 NKJ

"Again I say to you that if two of you agree on earth concerning anything that they ask, it will be done for them by My Father in heaven." Matthew 18:19 NKJ

Ministry Unlimited

Don't let any condition intimidate you. Before you see a giant tumor, Siamese twins or a paralyzed soul, imagine yourself laying hands and successfully praying for the worse condition you can think of before it happens. God's viewpoint is life and we are here to take a stand and intercede on behalf for that kind of life. If you feel a pain yourself it could mean that someone else needs prayer in that area and not you (*it has no right to be in you or anybody else anyway*).

Use the anointing while the connection is present, don't give people time to stir up doubt within their mind. To shift momentum in a bigger service, allow those who have already been healed to testify; so they can encourage others with borderline faith by raising their expectations.

When you have prayed and seen faith on someone, tell them to do something that they could not do before. If they were deaf, converse with them until they are solid in getting their miracle. If someone is blind and they can only see a little bit (*Which is more than what they started with*), continue to work with them as they are receiving a little bit at a time (*working of miracles*). Connect while you can and teach them how to keep their connection and their miracle.

If someone falls to the floor experiencing the power of God, let them continue in His peace unless the Lord directs you differently. You may want to have someone break their fall if this is a usual circumstance for you.

"As soon then as he had said unto them, I am he, they went backward, and fell to the ground." John 18:6

"The guards shook with fear when they saw him, and they fell into a dead faint." Matthew 28:4 NLT

"Then the spirit screamed and threw the boy into another violent convulsion and left him. The boy appeared to be dead..." Mark 9:26 NLT

Even as Jesus healed blind people in at least three ways, each person is different. If you ask a blind person what they need prayer for, they may not have the faith to have sight but may just want prayer for a headache. It is always good to know so you will be in agreement with them and not extend their boundaries of faith. If you start with their headache the Lord may lead you to pray for their blindness or just overpower them with His healing virtue right there. Read the interview of Jesus;

"Two blind men were sitting beside the road. When they heard that Jesus was coming that way, they began shouting, 'Lord, Son of David, have mercy on us!' 'Be quiet!' the crowd yelled at them. But they only shouted louder, 'Lord, Son of David, have mercy on us!' When Jesus heard them, he stopped and called, 'What do you want me to do for you?' " Matthew 20:30-32 NLT

You want the person to keep their healing making sure they are discipled and stay away from habits or associates who drove them into their consequences. If a person is delivered from drugs, you may not want to send him to witness at a drug house until he is strong. If a person is healed from A.I.D.S. they should not go back to hang out with sexual immoral people.

"Afterward Jesus found him in the temple, and said to him, "See, you have been made well. Sin no more, lest a worse thing come upon you." John 5:14 NKJ

"For it seemed good to the Holy Spirit, and to us, to lay upon you no greater burden than these necessary things: that you abstain from things offered to idols, from blood, from things strangled, and from sexual immorality. If you keep yourselves from these, you will do well." Acts 15:28, 29 NKJ

"I meant that you are not to associate with anyone who claims to be a believer yet indulges in sexual sin, or is greedy, or worships idols, or is abusive, or is a drunkard, or cheats people. Don't even eat with such people." 1 Corinthians 5:11 NLT

We are ordained to act on God's behalf and we are His behalf. Remove skeptical people with oppressing spirits if you have to. Although the God in you is invincible, don't operate in the flesh and don't get a head of Him.

"Trust God from the bottom of your heart; don't try to figure out everything on your own. Listen for God's voice in everything you do, everywhere you go" Proverbs 3:5 MB

The proportion of miracles in your church will be in proportion to the seeds you have planted in that field. Because skepticism has prevailed in the church, the cooperate faith needed for miracles have increased. Your congregation will gravitate towards what you are feeding them, so you can decide on the harvest you want. Teach them to memorize healing scripture verses and demonstrate love and wisdom. Sing songs that incorporate the healing, mercy and power of God. If a pastor is not teaching his congregation how to gather the spoils that Jesus fought for, he may lead people into division.

"This is war, and there is no neutral ground. If you're not on my side, you're the enemy; if you're not helping, you're making things worse." Luke 11:23 MB

In the spirit, you stand in a place to receive prayer. People all over the world are interceding for you. Prayers never die so we can step into the manifestations of prayers that have been prayed in intercession for thousands of years ago. As the body of Christ is today, the miracles and manifestations are coming to pass at an exponential rate with so many millions praying with faith to make things rapidly come to pass.

"And five of you shall chase an hundred, and an hundred of you shall put ten thousand to flight: and your enemies shall fall before you..." Leviticus 26:8

Paul had the power to enable the faith of others to believe. His meditation on how to deliver the words and convince others for long periods of time enabled him to maintain and strengthen his own faith above others around him. Sometimes against their own will. Even venomous snakes fell at his feet. There is no reason to fear anything. The shadows of death are just shadows. In some places where a crowd is not craving on the God man in you with cooperate faith you have to depend on Him to use your own anointing.

"Then Paul went to the synagogue and preached boldly for the next three months, arguing persuasively about the Kingdom of God...This went on for the next two years, so that people throughout the province of Asia—both Jews and Greeks—heard the word of the Lord. God gave Paul

the power to perform unusual miracles. When handker-
chiefs or aprons that had merely touched his skin were
placed on sick people, they were healed of their diseases,
and evil spirits were expelled" Acts 19:8-13 NLT

"One day as we were going down to the place of prayer,
we met a demon-possessed slave girl. She was a fortune-
teller who earned a lot of money for her masters. This
went on day after day until Paul got so exasperated that
he turned and said to the demon within her, 'I command
you in the name of Jesus Christ to come out of her.' And
instantly it left her." Acts 16:16, 18 NLT

"...The people of the island saw it hanging from his
hand...But Paul shook off the snake into the fire and was
unharmed." Acts 28:4, 5 NLT

"God doesn't want us to be shy with his gifts, but bold
and loving and sensible." 2 Timothy 1:7 MB

"Yea, though I walk through the valley of the shadow of
death, I will fear no evil; For You *are* with me." Psalm 23:4
NKJ

God's Word is not to show you what you don't have.
The Word confirms to the 'whosoever' people who will take
His Word at face value to dominate the planet. Signs and
wonders are meant for you. You've got high faith. You have
ever increasing faith. You don't have to be in Egypt saying
remove me from the drought, but learn to speak to the rock
and watch for the water come out. Tap into the supernatural power within you. Learn to flow with Him, to fulfill the
needs of the planet.

"But Jesus looked at *them* and said to them, "With men this is impossible, but with God all things are possible." Matthew 19:26 NKJ

God's boldness will come upon you to help others out automatically when you flow with the anointing. Keep your of confidence and trust in Him. Don't look at the circumstances and throw the promise out the window. There is no other way to please Him but by faith. Those of us who are in Christ, we have been given the nature and character of Jesus to do greater works. Your faith may not be that great yet, but you may have to start with 'Lord, help my unbelief' or Lord, I believe a little bit, but help me with the parts I have been taught to doubt. Surround yourself with people who believe on a higher level and teach those who fall short of the glory of God.

"...the father cried, "Then I believe. Help me with my doubts!"" Mark 9:24 MB

Potential miracles are waiting to happen whenever you enter a room. The undeniable power that's within you will exalt God's report over man's report. Someone before you who tried it and it didn't seem to work or were not sure when they asked may have regressed, but you will patiently continue in the understanding of his strength. You know that absolute truth is above every other truth. Some situations may be '*a*' truth, but He is the truth. His name reigns above problems and circumstances. His name carries the devil dusting power that will have your enemies at peace with you. You don't have just a piece of Jesus, you have the full indwelling. Accept the truth before you see evidence. I stand in agreement with every reader who wants manifestations in their lives!

"When people's lives please the Lord, even their enemies are at peace with them." Proverbs 16:7 NLT

"Nor is there salvation in any other, for there is no other name under heaven given among men by which we must be saved." Acts 4:12 NKJ

"For everyone who asks receives, and he who seeks finds, and to him who knocks it will be opened." Luke 11:10 NKJ

CHAPTER 14

Creative Miracles

I n the beginning there was something wrong with the earth

"...Earth was a soup of nothingness, a bottomless emptiness, an inky blackness." Genesis 1:2 MB

The darkness of the world attempted to deceive man into giving up something that was rightfully his. After Adam had fell, the idea of restoration was so far from his condemned thought life, that it took thousands of years for his seed to realize the original potential and power of the mercy of God. Even in recent years, thousands of congregations still have not believed the loving desire and will of God's heart. And even as powerful as the words in this book are, the enemy will try to snatch it away from you as soon as you read it.

"The farmer plants the Word. Some people are like the seed that falls on the hardened soil of the road. No sooner do they hear the Word than Satan snatches away what has been planted in them." Mark 4:14, 15 MB

"Keep vigilant watch over your heart; that's where life starts." Proverbs 4:23 MB

Saints are called to do miracles and show proof of a living God. When you doubt the *'doubter'* and stick to the truth of the word, you will help others to experience the victory. When you refuse to quench the Spirit with circumstances, people or opinions, the over comer in you will manifest each time. As a doctor is trained to help with cures for the body, we are endowed with unlimited power to help God's children.

"But you belong to God, my dear children. You have already won a victory over those people, because the Spirit who lives in you is greater than the spirit who lives in the world." 1 John 4:4 NLT

"Quench not the Spirit." 1 Thessalonians 5:19

Some may think back to the days of Job when the sons of God presented themselves and Satan did also. But the enemy will still try to be present when the word goes forth to give you a 2nd opinion. Satan will give you compromising things to compare with the word and see if you'll settle for a worldly consolation prize. But we can rejoice in knowing that the spirits are subject to us.

"...in this rejoice not, that the spirits are subject unto you; but rather rejoice, because your names are written in heaven." Luke 10:20

If we are called in Adam to subdue and replenish the earth, our dominion can begin in the present time by gathering the spoils from an enemy that has been defeated long ago. You can believe this even if other Christians have failed to fully accept this revelation. His power is not limited to headaches or traveling mercies. It's not harder for Him to heal cancer than a stomach ache. The limb growing, dead-man raising, creative miraculous resident power is within you. When God puts this word in you He gives you the ability to believe it. You are not intimidated by anything the enemy has to offer. God has given you the authority to replenish the earth quickly.

"Assuredly, I say to you, whatever you bind on earth will be bound in heaven, and whatever you shall loose on earth will be loosed in heaven. "Again I say to you that if two of you agree on earth concerning anything that they ask, it will be done for them by my Father which is in heaven." Matthew 18:18, 19 NKJ

We are created to show what the hope of His calling is, which are all enemies under the feet of the body of Christ. Our Father has seen the plan for us from the beginning a former rain and He waits for the latter rain.

"...I am God, and there is none like me, Declaring the end from the beginning, and from ancient times the things that are not yet done, saying, My counsel shall stand, and I will do all my pleasure" Isaiah 46:9, 10

"And the God of peace shall bruise Satan under your feet shortly..." Romans 16:20

"Therefore be patient, brethren, until the coming of the Lord. See *how* the farmer waits for the precious fruit of the earth, waiting patiently for it until it receives the early and latter rain." James 5:7 NKJ

It's not about us waiting for God to move. Jesus doesn't need to do any more than He already has. It's about the rain that flows from our hearts. It's about the creative and majestic power of our words to the Lord's chosen generation that believes on him.

"He who believes in Me, as the Scripture has said, out of his heart will flow rivers of living water." John 7:38 NKJ

We don't have to think '*that was Jesus or that was Paul*' because we have the same Spirit in us that kept Jesus from staying in the grave. We are highly recommended by God and chosen to do greater works. We are here to imitate God and follow his example. If we decide between the bible and the common word of the world, or if we think we have less authority then Jesus; we fall out of agreement with the word to be co-laborers with Him.

"...be imitators of God [copy Him and follow His example], as well-beloved children [imitate their father]." Ephesians 5:1 AMP

"For we are God's fellow workers..." 1 Corinthians 3:9 NKJ

Healing is like money in the bank. Creative miracles are requires different kind of handling and usually different meditation verses you can use to encourage yourself in the Lord. A creative miracle requires believing God's word and the immediacies of His present power through you. Our body parts in fullness were written in His book;

"Christ...existed before anything else, and he holds all creation together" Colossians 1:15, 17 NLT

"Your eyes saw my substance, being yet unformed. And in Your book they all were written…" Psalm 139:16 NKJ

"He restores my soul…" Psalm 23:3 NKJ

The world was framed only by faith and words. If a man is raised from the dust, stones can be raised to Abraham and cry out (Gen 2:7, Luke 3:8, 19:48), we can see the creative pattern that Jesus used to imitate God and show us how not to face reality, but create it.

"Then Jesus answered and said to them, "Most assuredly, I say to you, the Son can do nothing of Himself, but what He sees the Father do; for whatever He does, the Son also does in like manner. For the Father loves the Son, and shows Him all things that He Himself does; and He will show Him greater works than these, that you may marvel." John 5:19, 20 NKJ

"…God, who gives life to the dead and calls those things which do not exist as though they did." Romans 4:17 NKJ

Our bodies are in continuous creation. Science knows that the cells in our body regenerate approximately every 11 months. With creative miracles, you will speak cells into multiplication and turn on the physical DNA to the will and the power of God, because of the Presence in your words. Your ability to speak something out of nothing gives life and grows body parts. Even Adam did not have to wait for Eve to grow up into a woman. Will you confess *age and death* or power and life?

"The mouth of a righteous man is a well of life…" Proverbs 10:11

When you look at further creative miracles of Jesus, in the multiplication of fish and loaves, He first commanded the disciples and gave them an opportunity to do the same creative miracle;

"Late in the afternoon his disciples came to him and said, "This is a remote place, and it's already getting late. Send the crowds away so they can go to the nearby farms and villages and buy something to eat." But Jesus said, "You feed them ...."" Mark 6:35-37 NLT

I was able to witness this miracle on a missionary trip to Tecate Mexico. There were 6,800 people there in the stadium on the final day and we had enough for most of them. The food was multiplied to where many open hands received seconds and thirds and were satisfied. Around 400 people got saved and were sent to the local Pastors & churches there.

After six days God finished the earth. At the cross Jesus said "it is finished." The part of God we see active on this planet now is the Spirit through His body of believers. After the apostles had the Spirit come upon them, He took over in the lives of men everywhere. Even now He gives us power to become sons of God;

"Nevertheless I tell you the truth. It is to your advantage that I go away; for if I do not go away, the Helper will not come to you; but if I depart, I will send Him to you." John 16:7 NKJ

"But as many as received him, to them gave he power to become the sons of God, even to them that believe on his name" John 1:12

"Therefore those who were scattered went everywhere preaching the word." Acts 8:4 NKJ

We know that even now every enemy is obligated to bow the knee to the Word in us. The Presence of God is in our words. We were designed in His image. When we stop thinking like natural man and start thinking like God, we will share equal authority and will see equal results;

"Let this mind be in you which was also in Christ Jesus, who, being in the form of God, did not consider it robbery to be equal with God, but made Himself of no reputation, taking the form of a bondservant, *and* coming in the likeness of men...Therefore God also has highly exalted Him and given Him the name which is above every name, that at the name of Jesus every knee should bow, of those in heaven, and of those on earth, and of those under the earth" Philippians 2:5-10 NKJ

"I pray that your hearts will be flooded with light so that you can understand the confident hope he has given to those he called—his holy people who are his rich and glorious inheritance. I also pray that you will understand the incredible greatness of God's power for us who believe him. This is the same mighty power that raised Christ from the dead and seated him in the place of honor at God's right hand in the heavenly realms. Now he is far above any ruler or authority or power or leader or anything else—not only in this world but also in the world to come" Ephesians 1:18-21 NLT

The disciples showed power without the indwelling of God in them. Just think how much more now that we have the indwelling of God in us. We don't have this talent and power to keep to ourselves. We will make the creative replenishing of body parts to step up to the provision Jesus gave on the cross. There is nothing that the enemy has showed us that could be greater than the royal blood sacrifice of Jesus. The way of the Kingdom is ours.

"And I bestow upon you a kingdom, just as My Father bestowed *one* upon Me" Luke 22:29 NKJ

When we believe, we get what we say. We believe so we say it. The redeemed of the Lord can say so many powerful things knowing that the Lord will always back up the living Word.

"But since our spirit of faith is the same, therefore as it is written, I believed and so I spoke - I too believe and so I speak" 2 Corinthians 4:13 Mof

"Jesus was matter-of-fact: "Embrace this God-life. Really embrace it, and nothing will be too much for you. This mountain, for instance: Just say, 'Go jump in the lake'—no shuffling or shilly-shallying—and it's as good as done. That's why I urge you to pray for absolutely everything, ranging from small to large. Include everything as you embrace this God-life, and you'll get God's everything." Mark 11:22-24 MB

When our assurance, boldness and confidence is at the level of God's expectancy we can feel His presence ready to move or guide us into creative healing. We will look for those who desire to connect to the life changing power of God.

"Trust in the LORD with all your heart; and lean not on your own understanding. In all your ways acknowledge him, and he shall direct your paths." Proverbs 3:5, 6 NKJ

"When Jesus saw their faith, He said to the paralytic... 'I say to you, arise, take up your bed, and go to your house.' " Mark 2:5, 11 NKJ

The more people that are surrounding you with faith, the more effective you can be. According to corporate belief, Jesus could use the faith of the people for creative miracles. In a city with unbelief He only used the gift of healing.

"And because of their unbelief, he couldn't do any miracles among them except to place his hands on a few sick people and heal them. And he was amazed at their." Mark 6:5, 6 NLT

We will desire to see all healed, but we cannot always go beyond unforgiveness or a person's unbelief heal everyone. As previously discussed, their expectancy must be raised. I was in a hospital room and a young man with scoliosis could sense the presence of God upon me. (*It was not the presence that stays on you that disables you to function normally with people, but a super natural moving of the Spirit for those in need*). When he asked about the Presence, I told Him I talk am constantly talking with God and told him about His healing power. I noticed right away his faith was building. I told him; 'The Spirit is moving in your back right now, can you feel it?' and he said; 'Yes, I can feel it' and received a dramatic healing touch from the Lord. Give a person as much as they can handle while the anointing presence is upon you. Give them encouraging words to enjoy the Giver more than the gift and stay on the vine. Make sure God gets all the glory.
"I am the true grapevine, and my Father is the gardener. Remain in me, and I will remain in you. For a branch cannot produce fruit if it is severed from the vine, and you cannot be fruitful unless you remain in me. Anyone

who does not remain in me is thrown away like a useless branch and withers. Such branches are gathered into a pile to be burned. But if you remain in me and my words remain in you, you may ask for anything you want, and it will be granted! When you produce much fruit, you are my true disciples. This brings great glory to my Father." John 15:1, 4, 6-8 NLT

CHAPTER 15

Divine Health

Our bodies were not created to grow old. Through the fall of man became the availability of borrowing suffering, sickness and death. We are now more than ready to give it back. If our thoughts tell us that micro-organisms and germs are more powerful than the God, then fear gives greater power to the created than the creator. If we expect or have faith in health problems with changes in the environment, weather or plagues instead of the mercy of God, we will gravitate towards hopelessness and bondage. If we feel we are destined to die no matter how we pray or what the Word proclaims, we are in bondage. We are not under the law, but life.

"...he might destroy him that had the power of death, that is, the devil; And deliver them who through fear of death were all their lifetime subject to bondage." Hebrews 2:14, 15

"For <u>the law of the Spirit of life</u> in Christ Jesus has made me free from the law of sin and death." Romans 8:2 NKJ

The 'new man' within inspires the faith given to us. The blood of Jesus, The Name of Jesus and the Word of Jesus has redeemed us and overcome every spirit. The price has been paid with a 'check' written in blood before the foundation of the world, cashed in on Calvary, guaranteed by the Kingdom's government, and guarded by the King's army of angels for His royal priesthood children written in the Lamb's book of Life. We want to live the long life God has promised us and be around for our children and children's children; whether natural or spiritual children in the faith. Our spirit is connected to God for life through faith.

"For by me your days will be multiplied, And years of life will be added to you." Proverbs 9:11 NKJ

"Christ has redeemed us from the curse of the law, having become a curse for us (for it is written, *"Cursed is everyone who hangs on a tree"* Galatians 3:13 NKJ

"Every God-begotten person conquers the world's ways. The conquering power that brings the world to its knees is our faith." 1 John 5:4, 5 MB

"...To him who overcomes I will give to eat from the tree of life, which is in the midst of the Paradise of God." Revelation 2:7 NKJ

God's plan and desire for us is to live in divine health to fulfill His will. His nature is to preserve us and our new nature is to depend on him. The children of Israel experienced this walking in the wilderness; there was not a feeble one among them. There was preservation from hunger and thirst. Even the clothes they wore were preserved.

"Beloved, I pray that you may prosper in every way and [that your body] may keep well, even as [I know] your soul keeps well and prospers." 3 John 1:2 MB

"God said, "If you listen, listen obediently to how God tells you to live in his presence, obeying his commandments and keeping all his laws, then I won't strike you with all the diseases that I inflicted on the Egyptians; I am God your healer." Exodus 15:27 MB

"He brought them forth also with silver and gold: and there was not one feeble person among their tribes." Psalm 105:37

"Your clothes didn't wear out and your feet didn't blister those forty years." Deuteronomy 8:4 MB

Satan was the author of sickness and disease but now Jesus is the author and finisher of our faith. Our name is written in the Lamb's book of Life. And now that we have been saved from who we were, the Word continually teaches us about the abundant life available to us. We are His body that He wanted it to be glorified and whole even before there was a 'was'.

"And now, O Father, glorify Me together with Yourself, with the glory which I had with You before the world was." John 17:5 NKJ

Preservation also takes place in defense from weapons and people. "Hard to kill" apostles survived many attacks and prospered. The apostle John is good example of this; when they tried to boil him alive, he would not boil. So they sent him to prison where he wrote the book of Revelation.

And of course, the "Untouchable" Jesus would give death the 'slip' knowing what the opposition was up to.

"When a man's ways please the LORD, He makes even his enemies to be at peace with him." Proverbs 16:7 NKJ

"...They picked up rocks to throw at him. But Jesus slipped away, getting out of the Temple." John 8:59 MB

"They tried yet again to arrest him, but he slipped through their fingers." John 10:39 MB

"A thief is only there to steal and kill and destroy. I came so they can have real and eternal life, more and better life than they ever dreamed of." John 10:10 MB

The Word and the law of the Spirit of life has always been the same. Provision has always been available, as we see also in the Old Testament. Holy angels have protected God's chosen people from plans of fallen angels. An example of this is when the children of Israel walked by the red sea, accused God and Moses, and were bitten by snakes (Num 21:4-9). The poisonous snakes were always there (*even as evidenced in the same area in World War Two by the deaths of English soldiers*), but they spoke a *death sentence* unto themselves, because of an unchanging law that God had sent out before the foundation of the world (Deut 28:15-69).

"Jesus Christ the same yesterday, and today, and forever." Hebrews 13:8

The serpent that Moses put upon a pole would represent what Jesus would do centuries later, showing that wholeness was always his only plan, even if we make our own *(notice the snakes were still there to bite them, protection is not automatic, it requires faith).*

"And as Moses lifted up the serpent in the wilderness, even so must the Son of man be lifted up" John 3:14

You have life within you. You have a supernatural immune system. You're not a sponge for sickness, but you are here to provide healthy waves for miracles. Your belief and meditation on what the Word says will increasingly liberate you over the process of time. Your connection to eternal life is superior to any opposition. Your Spiritual diet will overrule your natural diet. Whether you eat manna or bacon, you need to seek and speak life.

"...Nothing will injure you." Luke 10:19 NLT

"...and if they drink any deadly thing, it shall not hurt them..." Mark 16:18

"Not what goes into the mouth defiles a man; but what comes out of the mouth, this defiles a man." Matthew 15:11 NKJ

"For every creature of God is good, and nothing to be refused, if it be received with thanksgiving" 1 Timothy 4:4

"Everything is clean to the clean-minded; nothing is clean to dirty-minded unbelievers." Titus 1:15 MB

The words out of your mouth should not claim things like '*this is my asthma*', '*I have diabetes*' or '*these are my allergies*' but change into confessions like 'this symptom may be *a* truth, but it's not greater than *the* truth', 'I have the promise, now I'm waiting on the manifestation' or 'by His stripes I am healed'. We have the choice to say things like '*I'm getting old and that's why I feel this way, or can't do these things, 'that's what happens when you get older'*, '*I am forgetting things because I am old'*. Mankind has a habit of claiming temporary illusions of the enemy. If the spirit of pain tries to get your mind into a '*make-believe'* state, you can fight the good fight of faith in victory by meditating on the promises of God. It may be '*a-truth'* that you are suffering, but when you know 'The Truth' it will make you free! If you don't know the Truth He can't do much for you. Your words carry a lot of power for you and others. A practice that I use is not to let someone speak negative words in my atmosphere without being checked. Your confession and/or the confession and faith you have in other people, will give you faith from either the Word of God, or opinions from men, medically educated or not.

"And ye shall know the truth, and the truth shall make you free". John 8:32

"Those who love to talk will suffer the consequences. Men have died for saying the wrong thing." Proverbs 18:21 Tay

"A gentle tongue [with it's healing power] is a tree of life, but willful contrariness in it breaks down the spirit" Proverbs 15:4 AMP

"...And every tongue *which* rises against you in judgment you shall condemn. This *is* the heritage of the servants of the LORD, And their righteousness *is* from Me," Says the LORD." Isaiah 54:17 NKJ

God wants to meet us on His level of expectancy and divine understanding. Choose how much light you want since the deficiency is never in God. Although diet and body exercise does profit, there is nothing like putting God's Word first and following the Spirit. We can choose to hold on to what millenniums of experience have to say or look for a promise in the Word written millenniums ago about our Lord and Savior who is no respecter of persons and says His promises are always yes (2 Cor 1:20).

If there is *ANY* sick among us, they should be able to go to the elders for prayer. Are you waiting on the Lord for the manifestation of His promise? Because God answers us abundantly more than we can ask or think, we need to prepare for more than what we expect.

"Is any sick among you? let him call for the elders of the church; and let them pray over him, anointing him with oil in the name of the Lord: And the prayer of faith shall save the sick, and the Lord shall raise him up; and if he have committed sins, they shall be forgiven him." James 5:14, 15

"Now all glory to God, who is able, through his mighty power at work within us, to accomplish infinitely more than we might ask or think." Ephesians 3:20 NLT

When we trust in the Lord with all our heart, we have confidence toward God to ask him for anything, when our heart does not condemn us. Now that we have forsaken our deceitful heart and received a clean one from the Lord, we silence the opinions of our flesh and wait on the Lord.

"Rely with all your heart on the Eternal, and never lean on your own insight; have mind of him wherever you may go." Proverbs 3:5, 6 Mof

"Whenever our hearts in [tormenting] self-accusation make us feel guilty and condemn us. [For we are in God's hands.] For He is above and greater than our consciences (our hearts), and He knows (perceives and understands) everything [nothing is hidden from Him]. And, beloved, if our consciences (our hearts) do not accuse us [if they do not make us feel guilty and condemn us], we have confidence (complete assurance and boldness) before God and we receive from Him whatever we ask, because we [watchfully] obey His orders [observe His suggestions and injunctions, follow His plan for us] and [habitually] practice what is pleasing to Him." 1 John 3:20-22 AMP

"The heart is deceitful above all things, and desperately wicked: who can know it?" Jeremiah 17:9

"Hide Your face from my sins, And blot out all my iniquities. Create in me a clean heart, O God, And renew a steadfast spirit within me." Psalm 51:9, 10 NKJ

A Look at the Old Testament displays God's will with the first deliverance. A word was given from God about an appointed time of our lifespan. If we are marked with an expiration date, we should learn how to handle our lives with care and prayer. Some walked into the promises of lengthened days because of the choices set before them, others knew better and did not.

"...I am the LORD that heals you." Exodus 15:26 NKJ

"Then God said, "I'm not going to breathe life into men and women endlessly. Eventually they're going to die; from now on they can expect a life span of 120 years" Genesis 6:3 MB

"And if you follow me and obey my decrees and my commands as your father, David, did, I will give you a long life." 1 Kings 3:14 NLT

"Now King Solomon loved many foreign women... In Solomon's old age, they turned his heart to worship other gods instead of being completely faithful to the Lord his God, as his father, David, had been. Solomon worshiped Ashtoreth, the goddess of the Sidonians, and Molech, the detestable god of the Ammonites." 1 Kings 11:1-5 NLT

After Abraham heard the promise of having a child at 100 years of age, he continued to have six more children after Isaac, being preserved to be 175 years of age (Gen 25:2, 3). At 120, Moses had good eyesight and preserved strength. In the Lamsa translation; it says his skin was unwrinkled (Deut 34:7). Saving power was also seen with Daniel and the Hebrew boys, who stayed in the secret place of the Most High; stopping the mouths of lions or being untouched by fire. We seen the body of Elisha well preserved after death, with enough life in his bones to raise the dead. When you hear and receive God's word, it will save you from the pit and keep you young and youthful.

"And the princes, governors, and captains, and the king's counsellors, being gathered together, saw these men, upon whose bodies the fire had no power, nor was an hair of their head singed, neither were their coats changed, nor the smell of fire had passed on them." Daniel 3:27

"My God sent His angel and shut the lions' mouths, so that they have not hurt me..." Daniel 6:22 NKJ

"Some time later, raiding bands of Moabites, as they often did, invaded the country. One day, some men were burying a man and spotted the raiders. They threw the man into Elisha's tomb and got away. When the body touched Elisha's bones, the man came alive, stood up, and walked out on his own two feet." 2 Kings 13:21 MB

"...he will be gracious and say, 'Rescue him from the grave, for I have found a ransom for his life.' Then his body will become as healthy as a child's firm and youthful again." Job 33:23, 24 NLT

After the flood, the Word for life from the giver set a standard at 120, even though God's friend Abraham lived to be 175 (Gen 25:7), and Sarah at 127 (Gen 23:1). After over 100 years, Abraham had more power than 'Viagra'. The lasting beauty of Sarah at 65 was still quite desirable by great rulers. Even in her 80's, the King of Gerar sent for her (Gen 20:2). At 90, she also nursed her son.

"So it was, when Abram came into Egypt, that the Egyptians saw the woman, that she *was* very beautiful. The princes of Pharaoh also saw her and commended her to Pharaoh. And the woman was taken to Pharaoh's house." Genesis 12:14, 15 NKJ

"Now Abraham said of Sarah his wife, 'She *is* my sister.' And Abimelech king of Gerar sent and took Sarah." Genesis 20:2 NKJ

To come into this fountain of youth and preservation we must follow the pathway of Jesus.

"Jesus said to him, "I am the way, the truth, and the life. No one comes to the Father except through Me." John 14:6 NKJ

"The fear of the LORD *is* a fountain of life, to turn *one* away from the snares of death." Proverbs 14:27 NKJ

"Hear, O my son, and receive my sayings; and the years of your life shall be many." Proverbs 4:9 NKJ

"For length of days and long life and peace they will add to you." Proverbs 3:2 NKJ

The fear of the Lord is the beginning of wisdom and the spiritual 'how to' for departing from the snares of the enemy. Wisdom is the attachment to the destiny of life and soul preservation. Whether we read in the word that tells us to 'honor mother and father' for long life, or staying away from greed or bad people (Proverbs 2:16-19, 4:10-14, 5:5, 28:16), we can make our own decisions to walk toward the fountain or a dry place. These dry places can also include stress, debt, unforgiveness or other things that curse our lives.

"'Honor your father and mother.' This is the first commandment with a promise: if you honor your father and mother, 'things will go well for you, and you will have a long life on the earth.' " Ephesians 6:2, 3 NLT

When we are unforgiving to another, regardless of the circumstances, this baggage detains us from the presence of God. In the same way, if we are not givers, we are cut off from peaceful prosperity.

"Honor the LORD with your possessions, And with the firstfruits of all your increase; So your barns will be filled with plenty, And your vats will overflow with new wine." Proverbs 3:9, 10 NKJ

"He who oppresses the poor reproaches his Maker, but he who honors Him has mercy on the needy." Proverbs 14:31 NKJ

"Will a man rob God? Yet you have robbed Me! But you say, 'In what way have we robbed You?' In tithes and offerings." Malachi 3:8 NKJ

Our lifestyle contributes to our well being. If we are envious our bones can suffer. If we overwork ourselves, we can suffer the consequences. Remember Jesus slept more than Jesus wept.

"A peaceful heart leads to a healthy body; jealousy is like cancer in the bones." Proverbs 14:30 NLT

"Because for the work of Christ he came close to death, not regarding his life, to supply what was lacking in your service toward me." Philippians 2:30 NKJ

If we curse others, cursing may come upon us, even unto our bowels. Don't judge or damn anything. The reasons why people go to hell are that they have committed sin against the creation in the world that God loves, or have not trusted the God who teaches how to love. Some of the same have received payment for the wages of sin upon the earth.

"He loved to curse others; now you curse him. He never blessed others; now don't you bless him. Cursing is as natural to him as his clothing, or the water he drinks, or the rich food he eats." Psalm 109:17, 18 NLT

"Do not judge others, and you will not be judged. 2 For you will be treated as you treat others. The standard you use in judging is the standard by which you will be judged." **Matthew 7:1, 2 NLT**

"But the fearful, and unbelieving, and the abominable, and murderers, and whoremongers, and sorcerers, and idolaters, and all liars, shall have their part in the lake which burneth with fire and brimstone: which is the second death." **Revelation 21:8**

"For the wages of sin is death; but the gift of God is eternal life through Jesus Christ our Lord." **Romans 6:23**

"Some men's sins are open beforehand, going before to judgment; and some men they follow after. Likewise also the good works of some are manifest beforehand; and they that are otherwise cannot be hid." **1 Timothy 5:23, 24**

God and His angels have power over fire. When you are in His will and following His Spirit, there is no fire that will burn you and no water that will overflow you, even if you have to walk on top of it. When we listen and obey the inner promptings of the Holy Spirit, we can avoid the trouble of all enemies, not just flesh and blood.

"And another angel came out from the altar, which had power over fire..." **Revelation 14:18**

"When you pass through the waters, I *will be* with you; and through the rivers, they shall not overflow you. When you walk through the fire, you shall not be burned, nor shall the flame scorch you." **Isaiah 43:2 NKJ**

"All the important people, the government leaders and king's counselors, gathered around to examine them and discovered that the fire hadn't so much as touched the three men not a hair singed, not a scorch mark on their clothes, not even the smell of fire on them!" Daniel 3:27 MB

"You serve me a six-course dinner right in front of my enemies ..." Psalm 23:5 MB

"When God approves of your life, even your enemies will end up shaking your hand." Proverbs 16:7 MB

"...no weapon turned against you will succeed..." Isaiah 54:17 MB

The Word is written for doers of the Word. You don't just want to listen to the Word. You want to hold on to it. You don't want to lose the provision like the children of Israel in the wilderness. If you miss the mark and sin, it opens up a door to the devourer. God wants us to stay healed. We must make the choice to continue in faith, so we won't lose our healing. Do not permit the devil to give you the same thing over and over again or try to bring back lying symptoms to you.

"But Christ, as the Son, is in charge of God's entire house. And we are God's house, if we keep our courage and remain confident in our hope in Christ." Hebrews 3:6 NLT

"...And Jesus said, "Neither do I. Go and sin no more." John 8:11 NLT

"But afterward Jesus found him in the Temple and told him, "Now you are well; so stop sinning, or something even worse may happen to you." John 5:14 NLT

"When an evil spirit leaves a person, it goes into the desert, searching for rest. But when it finds none, it says, 'I will return to the person I came from.'" Luke 11:25 NLT

"The Devil is poised to pounce, and would like nothing better than to catch you napping. Keep your guard up" 1 Peter 5:8 MB

Caleb held on to his fountain of youth knowing that he had a purpose in life that should be accomplished. While we are still on the earth, there is so much witnessing, evangelism, missionary work and intercessory prayer for us to do that we can't go up to heaven and do. Remind yourself that you are not here just for you, but your life here is to build the kingdom with the help and power of God. Take advantage of the long life God has provided for you. Don't be weary in well doing.

"...God has kept me alive, as he promised. It is now forty-five years since God spoke this word to Moses, years in which Israel wandered in the wilderness. And here I am today, eighty-five years old! I'm as strong as I was the day Moses sent me out. I'm as strong as ever in battle, whether coming or going." Joshua 14:10, 11 MB

It is God's pleasure for us to be in health and prosper. It gives Him glory and makes Him look like the provider and healer He actually is. When we see the light on a promise and continue to feed on it, we get stronger in the faith that pleases Him. I would rather have Him make me drink from a river more than a *'hit or miss squirt gun'* that says *'maybe God will let you live long or maybe He won't'*. His sheep that know His Word will be satisfied with a long life. Your goal to serve is backed up by the promise of heavenly protection that makes you invincible from the plans of the enemy;

"They are abundantly satisfied with the fullness of Your house, and You give them drink from the river of Your pleasures. For with You *is* the fountain of life; in Your light we see light." Psalm 36:8, 9 NKJ

"Yes, because God's your refuge, the High God your very own home, Evil can't get close to you, harm can't get through the door. He ordered his angels to guard you wherever you go. If you stumble, they'll catch you; their job is to keep you from falling. You'll walk unharmed among lions and snakes, and kick young lions and serpents from the path. "If you'll hold on to me for dear life," says God, "I'll get you out of any trouble. I'll give you the best of care if you'll only get to know and trust me. Call me and I'll answer, be at your side in bad times; I'll rescue you, then throw you a party. I'll give you a long life, give you a long drink of salvation!" Psalm 91:7-16 MB

"For the Lamb who is in the midst of the throne will shepherd them and lead them to living fountains of waters..." Revelation 7:17 NKJ

God wants to preserve you to be a witness. You are blessed to be a blessing. God gives seeds to the sower, and multiplies talents for the harvest. When you shower people with the fountain that you've been given, your fountain remains full of power. When John had quoted these examples from Isaiah (44:3, 55:1, 58:11), the prophecy that God would speak through men with His living water was fulfilled. If someone speaks to you with a different fountain than life, (i.e. *'you could go at any time'*) you should rebuke the thought and rebuke or refresh the person. He will give power to the faint and renew your strength. This is His idea and he wants us to get a hold of it. The conformation of youthful renewal in the Word *guides* us to get a strong hold on it. Faith has to be bigger than what you're experiencing or it wouldn't be faith. Pray for Godly youth, strength and wisdom. Pray off wrinkles or any other thing you may have previously associated with age. Some of us don't have faith in wrinkles, grey hair or dementia.

"Have you not known? Have you not heard? The ever-lasting God, the LORD, the Creator of the ends of the earth, neither faints nor is weary. His understanding is unsearchable. He gives power to the weak, and to *those who have* no might He increases strength. Even the youths shall faint and be weary, and the young men shall utterly fall, but those who wait on the LORD shall renew *their* strength; they shall mount up with wings like eagles, they shall run and not be weary, they shall walk and not faint." Isaiah 40:28-31 NKJ

"Who redeems your life from destruction, who crowns you with loving kindness and tender mercies, who satisfies your mouth with good *things, so that* your youth is renewed like the eagle's." Psalm 103:4, 5 NKJ

We who have received power to become the sons of God and partake of God's divine nature renew our mind and become like Jesus having all wisdom and understanding of the nature of God's healing and better yet, preservation for us.

"But as many as received him, to them gave he power to become the sons of God, even to them that believe on his name" John1:12

"For whom he did foreknow, he also did predestinate to be conformed to the image of his Son, that he might be the firstborn among many brethren." Romans 8:28

"For this cause we also, since the day we heard it, do not cease to pray for you, and to desire that ye might be filled with the knowledge of his will in all wisdom and spiritual understanding" Colossians 1:9

"The LORD preserves all them that love him..." Psalm 145:20 NKJ

Our confession changes from observations (*what happens when others have aged*) to revelation from the Word of what has been made available for us from the foundation of the world, from our God who is no respecter of persons. Jehovah Shamar. God preserves. Jesus saves. Seek and ye shall find.

"Then Peter replied, "I see very clearly that God shows no favoritism." Acts 10:34 NLT

"So I say to you, ask, and it will be given to you; seek, and you will find; knock, and it will be opened to you. For everyone who asks receives, and he who seeks finds, and to him who knocks it will be opened." Luke 11:9, 10 NKJ

"May God be merciful and bless us. May his face smile with favor on us. May your ways be known throughout the earth, your saving power among people everywhere." Psalms 67:1, 2 NLT

Being born and socialized in this world would have you filled with other reports other than God's report. Most of us have faith, but we have had some deep rooted unbelief crowding out the word. Unbelief comes from popular opinion, common circumstances, life experiences and impatience, mixed and multiplied with time, making us a target of the spirit of doubt and fear. But God has given us His opinion, put a death sentence on circumstances, gave us His life, patiently took the stripes, coming out of timelessness into time, to bring us out of all types of darkness, by the power of his Holy Spirit. <u>Because God loves you, He is giving you His Faith</u>. In these days of the corporate blessing to the body of Christ, it is getting easier to enjoy divine health now that we are hearing more messages about it. We believe God's report over every other report.

"Who believes what we've heard and seen? Who would have thought God's saving power would look like this?" Isaiah 53:1 MB

"And also that He might deliver and completely set free all those who through the [haunting] fear of death were held in bondage throughout the whole course of their lives." Hebrews 2:15 AMP

"For God hath not given us the spirit of fear; but of power, and of love, and of a sound mind." 2 Timothy 1:7

We know God's perfect will and desire is healing and long life for us all. Putting your trust in the Lord is refreshment to your bones, and health to all your flesh. Finding wisdom and getting understanding is a tree of life of peace, happiness and a longer, life without plagues or epidemics. Divine health becomes your expectancy.

"I don't want you to die, says the Sovereign Lord. Turn back and live!" Ezekiel 18:32 NLT

"Happy *is* the man *who* finds wisdom…length of days *is* in her right hand…" Proverbs 3:13, 16 NKJ

"It shall be health to your flesh, and strength to your bones." Proverbs 3:8 NKJ

This is your health plan. Your name is written in heaven, and God's will is being done in earth through you. The Yes has been written in heaven and is coming to all the earth which belongs to the Lord. Eternal life is now connected to you. Praise God. Go your way. Your faith will keep you whole.

The Word gives us abundant life with His eternal, resurrecting power within us. Our faith and desire in the possibilities of God, which can be impossibilities with men, aids us into crossing over unto the fountain of youthful strength. Enter into His rest and stay there.

**"...My purpose is to give them a rich and satisfying life."
John 10:10 NLT**

**"But test everything that is said. Hold on to what is good."
1 Thessalonians 5:21 NLT**

"For they are life unto those that find them, and health to all their flesh." Proverbs 4:22

CHAPTER 16

Greater Works

G od has ignited your heart with the fire to do greater works. The church was not made to just be a social club, but the body of Christ is here on His behalf and we are ordained to act on His behalf. Whether it is inside the walls of the church or outside of them, you have been validated by God to reach out and touch mankind with the love and power that God has invested in you. God is putting a demand on the anointing that He has placed within you.

"You didn't choose me. I chose you. I appointed you to go and produce lasting fruit, so that the Father will give you whatever you ask for, using my name." John 15:16 NLT

When you invite heaven into your life and become transparent for God to use you as a chosen vessel, heaven will move on your behalf. The angels of heaven wait for the prophesied leadership on the earth through you. The miracles will follow you like goodness and mercy all the days of your life. You will have what you believe. All the promises will manifest in the process of time and strategy of God. When God ways are put first, with the heart of evangelism and care for his people, we put ourselves into the blessing of Solomon (1 Kings 3-10-14). God has more than enough to take care of your needs.

"Surely goodness and mercy shall follow me all the days of my life…" Psalm 23:6

"And these signs shall follow them that believe; In my name shall they cast out devils; they shall speak with new tongues. They shall take up serpents; and if they drink any deadly thing, it shall not hurt them; they shall lay hands on the sick, and they shall recover." Mark16:19

"But my God shall supply all your need according to his riches in glory by Christ Jesus." Philippians 4:19

Again, The Word is for doers, not just hearers or readers. Don't just read this book and say that was good, unless you believe you are less than a conqueror or if you can only do a few things through Christ that strengthens you. Make up your mind now and look away from the pathway of destruction and choose life.

"And if it seems evil to you to serve the LORD, choose for yourselves this day whom you will serve…but as for me and my house, we will serve the LORD." Joshua 24:15 NKJ

We have the permit for heavenly activity on the planet. When you can see the vision that God is giving you, it will dictate how you will live this life. Jesus came to give you a plan for your life. He called you to win. He anointed you for greatness. His Spirit is permanently directing you to be fully persuaded of your leadership to the earth and His performance.

"Truly I tell you, whatever you forbid and declare to be improper an unlawful on earth must be what is already forbidden in heaven, and whatsoever you permit and declare proper and lawful on earth must be what is already permitted in heaven." Matthew 18:18 AMP

"If people can't see what God is doing, they stumble all over themselves; But when they attend to what he reveals, they are most blessed." Proverbs 29:18 MB

"For as many as are led by the Spirit of God, they are the sons of God." Romans 8:14

"And my speech and my preaching *were* not with persuasive words of human wisdom, but in demonstration of the Spirit and of power" 1 Corinthians 2:4 MB

"And being fully persuaded that, what he had promised, he was able also to perform." Romans 4:21

You are not designed by God to carry unforgiveness, guilt, debt and other things. You were designed in the Spirit and likeness of God. You were designed for results that you didn't have to wait for, or deal with the time realm. We weren't designed to sweat and labour for food, but called to call the fish out of school and on top of the grill. We have to cast our net on the 'other side of the boat... of time' The Word is nigh thee, even to multiply whatever you need to supply a camp of 5,000. When you know your Father always hears you, when you know that He said to ask anything in the name of Jesus and He will do it, you are ready. And really, I am likely just telling you what you already know, but you have keep hold of the truth and hold on to eternity.

"And whatever you ask in My name, that I will do, that the Father may be glorified in the Son. If you ask anything in My name, I will do *it*." John 14:13, 14 NKJ

All that God has given you will be stirred up to another level. God needs the fire He put in you to be brighter than ever before. He will take you where He promised you. Your faith is bigger than what you are experiencing now and God will make His vision your reality. God is calling pioneers to his army on a first come, first serve basis. Anything that seems big as a mountain will be moved by the Word of God. Eventually, no mountain will stand still underneath the Word. It may come from your mouth or another mouth.

"...for assuredly, I say to you, if you have faith as a mustard seed, you will say to this mountain, 'Move from here to there,' and it will move; and nothing will be impossible for you." Matthew 17:20 NKJ

"And the heaven departed as a scroll when it is rolled together; and every mountain and island were moved out of their places." Revelation 6:14

When we are led by the Spirit, we become sufficient and efficient (Acts 8:29, 11:12). Paul was sent by the Spirit to certain cities. God knew where the harvesting was needed the most. After his ministering, they came into the unity to be a cooperate blessing to others. Even when Paul was at Melita, 276 from the ship respected his word, and the corporate anointing helped to captivate the island even when those around Paul expected death. He used the immediacy of God's truth, which is better than fantasy. (*Fantasy is what people use when they choose not to listen to God*). Being in the right place at the Spirit led time, started the healing with a chief's father and led to many to get healed of their diseases.

"After they had come to Mysia, they tried to go into Bithynia, but the Spirit did not permit them. So passing by Mysia, they came down to Troas. And a vision appeared to Paul in the night. A man of Macedonia stood and pleaded with him, saying, 'Come over to Macedonia and help us.' Now after he had seen the vision, immediately we sought to go to Macedonia, concluding that the Lord had called us to preach the gospel to them." Acts 16:7-10 NKJ

"In the same quarters were possessions of the chief man of the island, whose name was Publius; who received us, and lodged us three days courteously. And it came to pass, that the father of Publius lay sick of a fever and of a bloody flux: to whom Paul entered in, and prayed, and laid his hands on him, and healed him. So when this was done, others also, which had diseases in the island, came, and were healed" Acts 28:7-9

Paul always prayed for boldness and solicited prayers for the elimination of any shyness, hindrance or hesitation to come upon him. He seemed to be ready for anything. When the kid fell out the window and died, there was no intimidation (Acts 20:9-12). Be on watch, for need to be ready when the Spirit wants to move on you for the behalf of others;

"But you, keep your head in all situations, endure hardship, do the work of an evangelist, discharge all the duties of your ministry." 2 Timothy 4:5 NKJ

You have prepared yourself as a willing vessel. You've given up your personal agenda for an intimacy with God when other people refused it for what the world has to offer. Expect the Almighty to move upon you to do great exploits and lead other people to experience healings, the immediacies of creative miracles and being raised from the dead.

Keep in mind the access of God in time of need. In special need times, we've seen Samson with supernatural strength (Judges 14:6, 15:15) and Elijah also, who built an altar, 'took out' 400 prophets of Bel and ran about 20 miles horse ahead of horse driven chariots (1 Kings 18:32, 33, 40, 46). These were new things in their lives, but God wants to do a new thing in yours and show you what to do. You are not limited to things happening in your life because you didn't see them in the bible.

"God is our refuge and strength, a very present help in trouble. Therefore will not we fear, though the earth be removed, and though the mountains be carried into the midst of the sea" Psalm 46:1, 2

"...I'm announcing the new salvation work. Before it bursts on the scene, I'm telling you all about it." Isaiah 42:9 MB

"The fact is, God, the Master, does nothing without first telling his prophets the whole story." Amos 3:7 MB

"When the Spirit of truth comes, he will guide you into all truth...He will tell you about the future." John 16:13 NLT

Speak with the confidence knowing that the power and presence of God resides in your voice. Your exhalation is holy. It has a special function to be a proof provider of a living God. Your voice will cast out cancer, deliver captives, and eject the bondages of depression, schizophrenia and suicidal tendencies. Your body even has the potential to walk on water when necessary. After Jesus resurrected, He right-fully claimed He has all power (Matt. 28:19). Our greater works are based on His Word to us. The word doesn't say as Jesus was, so are we, but "as Jesus IS so are we" (1 John 4:17). Be fruitful and glorify God.

"The Spirit of the Lord is upon me, for he has anointed me to bring Good News to the poor. He has sent me to proclaim that captives will be released, that the blind will see, that the oppressed will be set free, and that the time of the Lord's favor has come." Luke 4:18 NLT

"Most assuredly, I say to you, he who believes in Me, the works that I do he will do also; and greater *works* than these he will do, because I go to My Father. And whatever you ask in My name, that I will do, that the Father may be glorified in the Son." John 14:12, 13 NKJ

Also read "The Kingdom of God and Your Place in the Kingdom" by Jeff Lowe
Contact info: jdaniellowe@yahoo.com
Website: www.jdaniellowe.com

"The day before Jesus comes back."
A poem by Jeff Lowe

The bride will be ready,
  and yes equally yoked.   Rev 19:7, 2 Cor 6:14
Without spot or wrinkle,
  just as Paul had spoked.   Eph 5:27
Unity and one accord
  with all denominations,   Eph 4:13
The gospel of the kingdom being
  preached to all the nations!   Matt 24:14

All the saints are healed
  by the power of the Spirit   Acts 5:16
Demons going back to hell
  cause they don't wanna hear it.   Matt 8:29
satan's begging us to leave
  the damage has been done,   Col 2:15
All who dwell on earth
  will know the power of the Son! Rev 6:16

All who joined God's army will
  sing with one accord   Rev 15:3
The kingdoms of this world are
  now the kingdoms of our Lord.   Rev 11:15
Christs' body has matured, with
  full knowledge of God's will,   Eph 5:17,Col 1:9,Heb 5:14
To hurricanes, tsunamis;
  we'll just say 'peace be still!'   Mark 4:39,40

What more can we do?
  no demons left to fight,   1 Cor 15:22,23,26
The ex-cons, thieves and liars are
  `preaching 'God's alright'!   Titus 3:3,1 Tim 1:13
Abortion clinics shut down,
  our judges say 'God rules'   2 Thess 1:10
Our lives have become holy and
  prayers are back in school!   Eph 4:16

We've healed folks with our shadows,
    raised dead on ev'ry border,   Acts 5:15, Matt 10:8
Miracles are common place,
    we've got our house in order.   2 Tim 3:16,17
Wealth and riches in our house to
    take care of our poor,   Ps 112:3
Possessions shared, we've really cared,
    how could we ask for more?   Acts 4:32

Tommorrow all the people
    in the graves will hear His voice,   John 5:28
They'll rise up to the clouds,
    who've made Jesus their choice.   1 Thess 4:17,18
Even those who pierced Him,
    will see Him in the cloud,   Rev 1:7
And death will flee from those,
    so rebellious and proud.   2 Thess 2:11

Real hell on earth begins,
    that very frightful day,   Rev 9:6
As we watch from above,
    for the remnant we'll pray..   1 Tim 2:1
Until the time the Lord comes back,
    we'll rule and reign once more,   Rev 20:6
The knowledge of the Lord,
    will cover shore to shore!   Isa 11:9,10

And as I look today,
    many have caught the vision,   Prov 29:18
Learning that long time ago,
    the Lord had made provision.   1 John 3:8
Will you be a spectator,
    or walk the wilderness?   Josh 24:15
Or will you put on God's armour
    & teach those how to dress.   Eph 6:11

Apostles, prophets, teachers,
    are here for our perfection,   Eph 4:11,1 Cor 12:28
Keep minds, hearts and ears open,
    for spiritual direction!   John 14:26,16:13
And in that Eve when Jesus comes,
    I'll intercede once more,   1 Sam 12:23
For one more soul to answer,
    the knock upon the door.   Rev 3:20